UNBROKEN AND UNBOUND

UNBROKEN AND UNBOUND

A Life Dedicated to God, Justice, and the South

∽

Horace Patterson, D.D.

NewSouth Books
Montgomery | Louisville

NewSouth Books
P.O. Box 1588
Montgomery, AL 36102

Copyright © 2007 by Horace Patterson.
All rights reserved under International and Pan-American Copyright Conventions. Originally published with the ISBN 1-58838-055-6 by NewSouth Books, a division of NewSouth, LLC, Montgomery, Alabama.

ISBN-13: 978-1-60306-030-1
ISBN-10: 1-60306-030-8

Design by Randall Williams
Printed in the United States of America

With humble dedication

to my many honorable and loyal supporters

who have taught me that the best friends

are those who have been tested

by tide and time

Contents

	Preface 9
1	Beginnings 15
2	Called to Preach 22
3	Preparation For Leadership 33
4	Talladega, Alabama 56
5	The Board of Education 78
6	The Man Who Should Have Been School Superintendent 101
7	A Test of My Resolve 143
8	City Hall in Crisis 156
9	Who Is Jerry Jackson? The Mayor's Explanation 163
10	Leading and Learning 189
	Index 195

Photos follow page 100.

Preface

ON WEDNESDAY, August 30, 1995, the headline of the local Talladega, Alabama, newspaper read: "Patterson not just a politician, He's Also Pastor, Educator, and Writer." The article went on to say "Dr. Horace L. Patterson Sr. is a man of many talents, not the least of which is his ability to appeal to the voters. In the recent city election in Talladega, Patterson received 73 percent of the votes over two opponents to win another four-year term as city councilman. He was the only incumbent to be reelected."

In the first official council meeting in October of 1995, I was elected president of the Talladega City Council. My reelection coupled with my election as president of the City Council in a small southern town that maintains a majority vote over African-Americans is not only historically remarkable, it is racially promising and culturally enlightening. This is a story about wisdom and jealousy and how wisdom prevailed. It is a story about overcoming the worst kind of bigotry and the most dangerous Judases. Some people, both black and white, have worked together through the years to keep the races apart in general and the black community fragmented in particular. This practice is alive and well today. It is a formidable foe, but it is not indefatigable. It is a dangerous enemy, but not an unconquerable opponent.

These purveyors of smoke screens know what buttons to push and what strings to pull in order to keep whites and blacks fighting a battle that is often economically beneficial to a select few. It is much cheaper to elect a person to whom you can pay ten thousand dollars to personally, than deal with someone who will require that you spend a half million dollars providing streets, sewage, water, and protection services to the masses. It is no accident; it is by design that potential leaders, both white and black, who seek to replace the old selfish and retarding systems of a racially polarized society with groups of people pitted against one another by opposing interests are aggressively and cruelly dealt with.

The one great institution that has a mandate to overcome this eventual genocide is the black church. It is, therefore, forever under attack by those forces that seek to control it if they cannot destroy it and the leadership that it produces. No lie is too vicious, no plot is too evil, for these forces of division, hatred, and personal gain to set in motion. They must not win because if they do the rest of us will lose.

There are reasons why old issues continue to cloud our future. Petty criticisms from petty people may well be too simplistic a response to the people and pressures that divide, weaken, and distract us. Most of the Southerners who fought and died in the Civil War had no slaves, nor the potential to ever own slaves. Yet they fought. Many fought to their deaths for a way of life that brought financial gain to only a few families. Many of the strategies developed to combat racism and mobilize the strength of a community in need, have been neutralized by "foxes in the hen house"—misguided cut-throats who think they will somehow profit from their underhanded actions, never realizing that their participation is self-defeating. Some of these people will never change. Some will never see the big picture: their shortsightedness creates a barrier to impede the progress of their own children.

That's bad, but it's not fatal. My story is a reminder that hope is something nobody can take from you as long as you refuse to give it up. Dr. Rick Warren says, "It only takes God six hours to grow a mushroom, but it takes him sixty years to grow an oak tree." My faith has not become an oak tree but, thank goodness, it has grown larger than a mushroom. It has grown across the years through sorrow, suffering, setbacks, and setups. I tell you this story because it is the story of a man who knows that dead ends, dirty tricks, and disconcerting delays need not comprise the final chapter of any worthwhile pursuit.

I have seen good come out of evil and right come out of wrong. It is not a comfortable sensation to have to weave one's way through sinister and menacing mazes, yet it is by that activity the heart is made strong and the spirit is made courageous.

To see some of your goals and dreams dart past with swift wings and feel ridicule sweeping over your soul with quivering cries is hard, but sometimes necessary to foster the kind of growth that no one can afford to lose.

Unbroken and Unbound

I

Beginnings

IT WAS A HOT Saturday afternoon in July of 1963. The bases were loaded in the ninth inning, two outs. It was my turn at bat. We were behind by two runs. I had been in a horrible hitting slump and had gone from lead-off batter to hitting sixth. I was sixteen, playing baseball with a team of men twenty-one years old and older. We were the Paul Hill Tigers. We lived in a small community in Bessemer, Alabama, where there were two Saint Paul Baptist churches. Old Saint Paul was at the top of the hill, and New Saint Paul was at the bottom. New Saint Paul had split from Old Saint Paul, and the split in the churches also reflected a division in the community. All of my other teammates were members of Old Saint Paul. I was the only member of New Saint Paul to make the team.

It was strange, but even as I made my way to the batters' box, I sensed hostility, not simply from the other team, but from my team members as well. For you see, I had come to a place of great possibility. I had reached a station that was pregnant with the potential for community praise. The team that we were playing had been one of the best in the Birmingham area. As a matter of fact, several of their players had been drafted by the Birmingham Black Barons and the Bessemer Rough Rocks. These teams were semi-pro black baseball teams that enjoyed legendary status in our community.

I am amazed that the good Lord uses many common things to

fashion out character. And as I reflect upon it, it seems to me that the God who used a slingshot in David's life started a process in mine through a prized bat in the ninth inning of a baseball game. As I made my way to the batters' box, I saw disgust and disapproval on the faces of some of my own teammates. This had not been created by my batting slump. It had more to do with my chance for glory than it had to do with my recent frustrations. It came from a mindset that would rather lose the ball game than secure a victory won by a member of New Saint Paul.

It escalated out of a foolish yet prevalent spirit that I would have to confront for the next thirty-five years of my life. From that dusty, humid Saturday afternoon, I was introduced to an adversary that I would later face while seated on cushioned pews under massive church windows, in formal halls of government, on the campuses of stalwart academic institutions, and inside eloquently decked boardrooms. Some people would rather attend a pity party than celebrate a common victory, if they can prevent a certain person from getting the credit.

I walked past the scornful faces on that Saturday afternoon back in 1963. I made my way from the batters' circle, and before I could step up to the plate the first-base coach, Lee Booker, called a time-out. He walked over to me. Lee was a good guy, but the other team members had put pressure on him.

He said, "If they pitch close, let the pitcher hit you and take a walk."
I said, "What if they don't?"
He replied, "Remember what you told me about that impala?"
I smiled. I remembered.
Then Lee said, "If they throw you strikes, you don't have to swing."
"Yeah, I know, but I don't want to be an impala."
He smiled. He knew what I had in mind.

In 1960 my parents bought a brand new Chevrolet Impala. I was curious about the word "impala." I researched the word and I found out that the impala is an African antelope. The African impala can jump more than ten feet high and can travel more than thirty feet in a single leap. It can run as fast as fifty miles an hour. However, in spite of its jumping, leaping, and running ability, there are African impalas kept in zoos all over the world inside a three-foot wall. The reason is simple—the impala will not jump if it cannot see where its feet will fall. It has no faith. It is scared to take a chance on what might or might not be. Its unwillingness to take a chance results in an isolation that is largely self-imposed.

I had shared this story about the African impalas with Lee one day as I drove to the store. I recall telling him, "I drive an Impala, but I'm never going to be one."

My time had come. I clicked my shoe spikes to rid them of dirt, dug in, and waited for the pitch. My heart raced, my pulse quickened, my hands grew cold, my mouth grew dry, and my stomach rolled. I was scared and yet I was excitedly, magnificently, and energetically alive.

The first pitch was a low fast ball. I saw it, swung, and missed badly. Then he wasted a pitch high and outside. I took it for ball one. Another pitch roared down in the dirt . . . ball two. My mind started thinking and my heart started hoping for a walk. But then it happened, a high curve ball hung in the air that seemed to whisper, "Hit me." I did; a triple into deep right field. One run scored, two runs scored, and then Daniel made the turn from third to home. He scored. Safe! And we won.

Even my detractors got caught up in the celebration, and the amazing thing that I learned on that day is that if you don't break, nobody can trash you. The hit was great, but even if I had gone down swinging or hit into a forced play, I knew that I had gone after a hitable pitch. I did my best. I took a chance and even my critical teammates, if only for a brief while, enjoyed a team victory more than they focused on the praise that might have been raised on my behalf. I didn't whine about their team spirit. I simply stepped up, stayed up, batted up, and we won. My slump did not matter. Even the talent of the opposing team didn't matter. It only made our victory sweeter.

Somehow it hit me. When people have no victories to celebrate, they let their differences become fences that separate rather than gates that open up potential for something a whole lot better than what they have. The sense of celebration was great, but short-lived in my world. In just a matter of days we did to ourselves what no team, force, or race of others could have done to us. The feeling seemed to have spread through the team that somebody needed to blow out my candle in order for theirs to shine brighter and before long, instead of becoming a better team, we put our own fire out.

Somebody said, "Yeah, Horace got the hit, but the pitcher was tired. He had pitched two days in a row."

Betty Smith thought I was cute when I was popular, but before long she told some of my friends, "He's got the big head, just like them other folk at New Saint Paul."

Hence, life went back to a state of fragmentation. I continued to drive the Impala whenever I was allowed to, but even as I drove it and admired it I became more determined that I would never become or let anybody make me into an African impala.

At five feet six inches and never weighing more than one-hundred and forty pounds in high school, stark determination made up on the baseball field what I lacked in size and power.

As a shortstop throwing with my right hand and batting from my left side, I learned to aim for hits and not home runs. With a quick stroke, I connected to all fields with an assured regularity.

At the age of seventeen, I made the roster of the Bessemer Rough Rocks. The long evenings of practice and the agony of seeing my errors magnified by my peers and welcomed by my adversaries paled on the day I received my uniform of navy stripes woven against a white background. That uniform had the smell of moth balls. I closed my eyes and covered my face with my uniform shirt and savored the moment as one might relish the taste or smell of fine food or drink.

My selection to the team did not happen without some second guessing. My Uncle Curtis (Curt for short) Jordan had been the owner of the Bessemer Rough Rocks baseball park for ten years.

Uncle Curt was a large muscular man with dark skin who sported several gold teeth. His hands were callused from years of swinging a pick and manning a drill in the coal mines of Bessemer and Birmingham. His eyes were often red and tired from years of exposure to the ore dust and particles that saturated his world of work. He had very little formal education, yet he demonstrated an uncanny ability to analyze the times in which we lived. "Things are gonna change. I wish I was a young man again," he often said as he habitually stoked his silver mustache and brushed his salt and pepper hair waves which were produced by a nightly routine of wearing a stocking cap.

Uncle Curt and his wife, Aunt Mary, who was a soft-spoken and reserved mulatto-skinned woman, had no children of their own. I spent most of my high school years in their home which was located only a block from our family homestead. At times they could be extremely generous, but their generosity often came with strings attached. They were emotionally isolated by several of our family members, including, at times, my father.

"Your Uncle Curt is a pretty good fellow most of the time," said my dad to me on several occasions. "You just have to feed him and Mary from a long-handled spoon."

Uncle Curt took great pride in my baseball accomplishments, as he vicariously lived out a portion of his own childhood dreams. He and I often clashed. He wanted me to hit clean up. I wanted to be a lead-off batter. He wanted me to become another Willie Mays and play center field. I just wanted to stay at shortstop. He drove me to be my best even as I, more often than seldom, recoiled at his insistence. By the time I was seventeen, my father had died and Uncle Curt was the most stable adult male figure in my life.

There are days in our lives when a single act sends forth such change that life for us is never quite the same, when one moment acts as a pebble thrown into the wade-pools of our lives, sending ripples through years of our existence. A moment that dictates as it changes, a singularity that reaches from its occurrence to affect everything that comes after. That moment came for me in 1964.

One balmy Friday afternoon in August as we practiced for our next ball game, a group of white guys showed up at the park. They asked us if we wanted to play a practice game. One tall sinewy fellow with bright red hair seemed to be their leader. He looked us over with an arrogance that elicited my anger and said, "We'll even give you boys the first bat!" Before

I could speak, Git Wilson, the manager of our team said, "Thanks, but we are finished practicing for the day." The white guys left. I was angry with Git, but I knew better than to say anything. My baseball life was perfect and at that time in my life when baseball was perfect, just about everything else was too. However, before the night was over I was destined to learn the error of placing all your happiness in something that people can take away.

I was fast asleep. It was 11 p.m. and my Aunt Mary awoke me. She was crying. "Somebody has burned down the ball park," she said. I sprang up, startled as if I had been hit by a brick rather than shaken from my sleep. Aunt Mary's tears arrested me. I had never seen her cry before. She frantically repeated the news as best she could through her tears and attempts to catch her breath.

I couldn't believe it even though the tears of Aunt Mary validated the tragedy. I hurriedly rubbed the sleep from my eyes and with quivering hands, I dressed myself and headed for the park. It was normally a fifteen minute drive. I don't know whether time crept slowly for me that night or if it passed swiftly as I headed for the park in my '55 Chevy.

The closer I got to the park, the more clearly I could see the death of a major source of my joy and self-esteem. I knew that we did not have insurance. Uncle Curt had complained that he had tried to buy fire insurance for the park, but no agency would insure it.

The rising flames roared against the empty void of one of the darkest nights I'd ever known. It was a suffocating, sweltering spectacle. The heat from the flames was oppressive. Uncle Curt was there when I arrived. Git Wilson and most of the Rough Rock team members stood and stared angrily as police cars arrived and parked. Policemen pointed and pushed the steadily swelling crowd away from the burning inferno.

The fire department arrived late and claimed that the burning tiers of seats and the rows of vertical planks that made up the fence were too far gone, even though we could see parts of the wall standing erect untouched.

"Why are they just standing there?" I asked as I walked up to one of the policemen. Before he could answer and before I could speak further, a strong hand gripped my shoulder and quickly yanked me from the presence of the policeman. It was Uncle Curt. He spoke to the policeman and said, "Sir, he didn't mean any harm. He's just upset." The policeman replied, "You better teach that boy some manners before he gets all of y'all in a lot of trouble."

It was 1964. The entire police and fire entourage was white. At that time we were not even black. We were "Negroes" to ourselves and "colored" was the most respectful label that we could expect from most white people in Bessemer and Birmingham.

Uncle Curt told me to go to my car, sit there, and keep my mouth shut. I did for a while, but after a few minutes I looked out and saw a truckload of white guys. I recognized the red-headed guy driving the truck. It was the same guy that had wanted to play us in a practice game. He looked at me and laughed triumphantly. Git Wilson and three of the men from our team started to walk toward their truck, but they meandered their way into the presence of the policemen.

Git Wilson followed them and told the policemen about our earlier encounter. One policeman spoke and said, "Y'all ain't got no evidence. Don't y'all know that these men can sue y'all for slandering their good name? Y'all best go home before somebody here ends up going to jail and I'm telling you it won't be these white men."

It was 1964 and Uncle Curt said that he was too old to start over. He didn't have the money and even if he had had the money, he no longer had the will. He was never the same after the fire. We talked, but never about his sense of helplessness nor about my sense of loss.

Integration had come to baseball, yet there were many black teams who continued to play among themselves. I was scouted by the Kansas City Monarchs and I had given some serious thinking to a professional baseball career. "Hammering" Hank Aaron's first game as a Milwaukee Brave saw him go 0 for 5. He kept at it. He didn't let that first game get him down. His name soon became a household word because of his devotion.

While I had the talent to play baseball, something happened to my devotion to the game. What had been my life simply became my hobby.

2

Called to Preach

CHURCH LIFE at New Saint Paul played a major part in my character development, but at no time did I ever want to be a preacher. Our church, like black churches everywhere, was not only our source of spiritual sustenance, but it was also our primary place of socialization. At that time in our history, we, as African Americans, only had two institutions—our church and our school. It is a sad commentary, but today, as we race toward the twenty-first century, the only institution we still have today is our church. And because this is the case, it is heartbreaking when I see the church take on the role of the African impala.

I never wanted to be a preacher. I wanted to be an attorney. The Bible stories of Moses delivering the Israelites from slavery coupled with growing up in Bessemer, Alabama, in the early 1960s seemed to usher me in that direction.

The injustice that escalated from and clearly produced (in my mind) the fiery destruction of our baseball park was bearable for me only because the church gave me the strength to endure and the counsel to overcome adversity. I had no illegal drugs then, nor did I need them. I was not in a street gang, nor did I want to be.

From Sunday school and Bible study lessons, I was taught and caught. I was taught that bitterness destroys bitter people. I was caught and held up by the strong arms of faith in a God who loves to make wrong things right. I was not taught to look to the television for guidance. I was led, fed, and bred by the tenet values that come from the church.

Silicosis

Most of the adult males worked in our community. It was expected. It was commonplace. I guess what would have been uncommon is for a healthy male to have been unemployed. Eighty percent of the working males in our community worked in the ore mines. This was a time before safety issues became dominant, and I can recall the hacking coughs even in church from fathers and older brothers dying from silicosis, a disease of the lungs caused by inhalation of silica dust found in the mines over a long period of time. These brave men worked hard. Many died too soon. Some became disabled only to suffer through old age.

I shall never forget the day that the community of retirees were told that the pension plan that they had had become a colossal financial disappointment.

The world and language of Wall Street, stock portfolios, capital gain distributions, real estate investment trusts, and dividends reinvestments were beyond these common and hard-working men's frame of reference. They had counted on receiving 250 dollars a month, but were arbitrarily told by mining company executives and attorneys that their maximum monthly benefit had been slashed to only thirty-five dollars a month.

With that sad and sudden news, a groping depression swept over many of them and a kind of vaulting unrest gnawed at their peace of mind as they contemplated an ominous financial future. I saw men who had walked proudly buckle under the weight of being called to pay up when they had nothing to pay down.

Whether the collapse of the pension plan was sparked by poor management or something more sinister, I cannot say. They had some community meetings, but they never forged a legal response to resolve their financial disasters.

In order to keep the wolf from their door, many with bucolic backgrounds merged their resources and resorted to, as well as embraced, the rich soil in rural areas of Jefferson county as an old friend turns with his needs to a trusted and faithful companion who can always be counted on when times are hard.

As creative and resourceful part-time farmers, they raised cotton, corn, beans, greens, okra, potatoes, and watermelons in order to make ends meet.

As I listened, watched, worked, and prayed for these disappointed but ultimately undefeated men, I felt that I could best help them by becoming an attorney. I wanted to sue the mining company. Silicosis robbed me of my father. He had died of the disease, and I was unable to help him. I wanted to honor his memory by helping others.

Billy Blount

I lived in Bessemer. I was bussed to Wenonah High School in Birmingham. Billy Blount was one of the "baddest dudes" in school. He couldn't read well, he couldn't count and he drank cough syrup to get high. Nobody messed with Billy Blount—not the teachers, or even "House Cat." I can't remember his real name, but House Cat used to smoke behind the gas house at Wenonah, where they kept the gas for the school buses. Nobody checked for smokers near the gas house, because the teachers felt like nobody would be nuts enough to smoke there.

House Cat was. House Cat did. House Cat would do anything except mess with Billy Blount. House Cat's greatest claim to fame happened one night at a Wenonah verses Parker High School football game. House Cat cussed at a white policeman in front of the cheerleaders. He ran. They caught him, beat him, and jailed him. But they didn't kill him. So when he got out he became a legend in his own time, not just at Wenonah, but everywhere. House Cat was a celebrity. But as tough and rough as House Cat was, he didn't mess with Billy Blount.

It happened before class. I was talking with Patricia Jeter. She was sweet and I was definitely interested. I didn't know that Billy Blount had a crush on her. Billy walked up, looked at me, and slapped me across the face. He didn't hit me hard physically, but it was a thunderous blow to my ego. I had to do something.

I walked off, went into a classroom, picked up a desk chair, and crowned Billy Blount on the head. I knew that he would probably kill me if I didn't go after him, so I jumped on him. I held him down. He pulled out a knife and cut my hand, but I refused to let go.

Finally, he looked up as I held his throat and said, "Y'all get this fool off me before I kill him."

What a line! I couldn't help but smile even though my hand was bleeding. Here's this guy I've smashed over the head with a chair, I'm sitting on top of him with my hands around his throat, and he tells the people around to save me! I couldn't stay mad. I knew Billy Blount's history. He had adults in his house, but he was on his own. He had never been taken to church. He had never been told to be home before ten. Nobody in his world protected him. He had been on his own.

I knew Billy Blount and a few other guys like him. I wanted to be an attorney because I knew that guys like Billy would always need some legal help. I knew that sooner or later Billy would get into something he couldn't get out of and he might not even make it unless he had some legal help. He was tough. He had hit me and even cut me, but I knew in my heart that Billy Blount was not bad by choice. He had become defensive because nobody loved him in his world. His meanness was his defense. Nobody messed with him, but nobody loved him either.

"Mama Look at Them Niggers"

During the early sixties, politicians in Alabama used the word "nigger" to get elected more quickly than they made promises to advance the state. I heard John Patterson run for governor promising "to keep niggers in their place." I remember the infamous "Segregation, Yesterday, Today, and Forever" speech by George Wallace. I stood in shock and wept when the bomb exploded in the Sixteenth Street Baptist Church in Birmingham that killed four innocent girls. I recall vividly the mean-spirited answer given by police commissioner Bull Connor in Birmingham when asked why he turned water hoses on black demonstrators. He gleefully said, "I washed them cause I don't want my dogs to bite no dirty niggers." I could not understand what we had done to elicit such hatred.

But one afternoon as three friends and I walked through an all-white community between Bessemer and Birmingham called Lipscomb, I was hit with a revelation that racism was born out of a culture that did not even know that it was wrong, let alone evil. Racism is both caught and taught, and sometimes those who are racist have no idea that their deeds are evil.

As we walked the main street of Lipscomb on our way home, a small white girl, probably about five or six years of age, called to her mother from the porch, saying, "Mama, Mama, look at them niggers." She laughed. The mother stared.

We pretended not to notice, but we couldn't help but hear. It was as if she were saying, "Look at the monkeys"—*Look at someone who is not someone. Look at something that is a thing and nothing more. It has eyes, feet, and a face, but it is not a person. It is just a thing to look at. To laugh at. It is not someone to get to know. It does not have feelings. It does not have deep-rooted emotions. It is, at best, a lesser creature. Do not give it respect; it does not deserve it.* Her words, and the thoughts that accompanied them, hurt.

We walked on. We went home. I don't even remember if we talked about it, but there is one thing I do remember, and that is we didn't do anything about it. We didn't even talk about what we could do to change a world that made six-year-old girls say, "Mama, Mama, look at them niggers." It was as if we accepted this evil.

Well, even if we did as a group, I didn't as an individual. I wanted to be an attorney. I wanted to erase laws that made segregation legal and Jim Crow comfortable. I wanted to take down that "White Only" sign located over the water cooler at F. W. Woolworth. I guess I ought to confess that on several different occasions I did break the law. I drank from a "White Only" water fountain, and I do believe that that water was a bit cooler during summer months.

Divine Intervention

My goals were admirable, my desires were good, but my life had already been planned. Anything that I tell you about the black church or about my call to preach is small compared to what I can't tell you. The supernatural is unexplainable. For two years I found myself experiencing both physical and spiritual enigmas. I began to sleepwalk at night. I had been a very healthy child, but I began having nosebleeds, headaches, and leg cramps to the point that I couldn't run my leg of the 440 track relay. It was a time when I had to discover God's "no" before I could respond to God's "go."

Gripped by an impulse that I could not define or dismiss, I became withdrawn and, at times, quite annoyed when questioned about my periods of self-imposed isolation. It is difficult to explain to others that which you do not fully understand yourself.

I found a refuge only in the sanctuary of silence, which strengthened my resolve to pursue the beckoning hand of a mysterious invitation that I could not, at that time, share with any other human being.

The Ministry of Dr. Martin Luther King, Jr.

My aunt never told me why she bought that record. One cold winter evening I returned from school to find that she had purchased an album by Dr. Martin Luther King, Jr. I still don't know why she bought it.

The album recorded his speech on having "Strength to Love." I had never been moved as that speech moved me. I spent countless hours playing and replaying it. I began to read everything I could find written about him. I listened to him on the radio and I watched him on television. I spoke to my pastor about his work.

He replied, "That man is going to get somebody killed and nothing will probably change." I went to school and the principal of our high school told us that we'd be expelled if we cut school and went marching. I slowly began to understand what Dr. King meant when he spoke about redemptive suffering.

As I dug deeper into the writings of Dr. King, I was given an insight into a book of the Bible that had not only puzzled me, but had also threatened me. It was the Book of Revelation. But as I searched for his speeches, sermons, and letters, I came across his profound message titled "Three Dimensions of a Complete Life." I still wanted to be an attorney, but something was happening in my heart when I read "John the

Revelator, imprisoned on a lonely, obscure island called Patmos, was deprived of almost every freedom, except the freedom to think." Dr. King went on to explain that a new city of God would be possible, a city that would not be an unbalanced entity with towering virtues on one side and degrading vices on the other. It would be complete on all sides.

It hit me like a rock. I didn't have the freedom to go to see the movies of my choice. I didn't have the legal freedom to use public bathrooms or drink from public water fountains, but I did have the freedom to quietly and prayerfully think. I had the freedom to think about all the good things our community represented and how those good things could and should have become better things. And the more I thought, the more central the work and ministry of the black church became in my mind, heart, and soul. But I still wanted to be an attorney.

As I read on I found myself convicted by Dr. King as he wrote: "This attempt to substitute a Man-centered universe for a God-centered universe leads only to deeper frustration. We sail upon the seas of modern history like a ship without a compass. We have neither a guide nor a sense of direction. We doubt our doubts, and wonder whether, after all, there may not in truth be some spiritual force undergirding reality."

In the black church, when a message convicts, we often use the phrase that it is "stepping on somebody's toes." The words of Dr. King didn't just step on my toes, they tap-danced over my feet. I wanted to do good. I wanted to help needy people. I wanted to make sure that old men suffering from silicosis had an advocate. I wanted to make sure that the racists in the state of Alabama had a foe. I wanted to stand in opposition to a culture that bred evil attitudes in the hearts and minds of six-year-olds.

There was one problem. I was man-centered. I might have had a map, but I wasn't in a desert. I was about to set sail upon my life voyage and I had no compass. I had no voice ringing in my soul saying, "This way!" As the months passed, I was no longer sure that what I wanted to be was what I needed to be.

A Stupid Fight

At a time when racist hatred was killing innocent little girls, setting people's homes on fire, and bracing itself for the ongoing, brutal fight ahead, I was busily trying to find answers. One of the things that deeply troubled me was that black people continued to hurt each other, even in the church. I don't know where it came from, but in the church that I attended and at others in my community, a strange and uncomfortable event often took place. If a girl or woman had a baby out of wedlock, she was required to come down the aisle, stand before the church, and make a public apology. I was young, but to me it seemed like an army attacking one of its wounded. This practice often ran the female away with a sense of shame that followed her in ways that bore "no fruits of repentance." The solitary figure of the already ashamed woman walking down the aisle was a sorry sight. Another thing that bothered me about the procedure was the double standard: the church never required the boy or man who had gotten the girl or woman pregnant to confess before the congregation.

While a generous and compassionate spirit has always marked the black church, there has also been in our church the potential for self-promotion. When people hit hard financial times, it seemed as if there was never enough money to help people on the spot. And even if there was money available, it could not be used until after a meeting was held by everybody or another public offering was taken. I always hated to see a family in need paraded before the church, saying they needed money to turn on their lights or to buy food. In order to get help, the needy always had to go through certain people or certain families in the church which created, at times, a mentality of kingdom-building rather than a true spirit of compassionate giving. It is possible to feed the hungry and starve the self-esteem.

At a time when the possibility of positive change permeated the air, there were still far too many indicators that old habits die hard. It was 6:30 p.m. on a Friday in April. New life pushed up from the ground in the form of green grass, blooming flowers, and growing trees. The phone rang.

"Horace?"

"Yes?"

It was Minnie Smith. "We need some of your preaching."

"Girl, what are you talking about? I haven't been preaching."

"Yes you have. You might not know or you might not call it that, but boy, you've been preaching and we need some of it tonight. Larry Johnson and Byrd Wilson are going to kill each other. You remember the other day when you told us that it was stupid for black people to shoot their own soldiers while they were in a war? You were right, but tonight at eight those two dummies are going to have a razor fight. Boy, you need to do some preaching."

"Where is the razor fight supposed to happen?" I asked.

"Over the hill next to the school."

I hung up the phone. I sort of laughed at Minnie's assessment of my interventions. I had never called it preaching. I just thought of it as helping. Regardless of what it was, I knew that I had to find a way to stop those two fools. They were first cousins, of all things. Stupid, just plain stupid.

By the time I reached the place for the razor fight, a group had already gathered. A razor fight was done with straight-edge razors. It was not just stupid, it was extremely dangerous. When I found out that the conflict was about some name-calling incident, I tried to lighten up the mood by telling a story about Abraham Lincoln. The idea was to get those two dummies to laugh at themselves. I hoped to diffuse the situation by calming Byrd and Larry down.

I stood between the two of them, in the midst of the small group of onlookers, and began to speak.

The story of Lincoln went something like this: Lincoln said people were always making fun of the way he looked. Sometimes it reminded him of the story of a man riding on his horse through the woods. One day an old lady stopped the man and said, "Sir, you must be the ugliest man I have ever seen."

The man replied, "Madame, you are probably right, but if I had another face, do you think I would leave home with this one?"

The lady said, "I know it's not your fault, but the least you could do for the rest of us is stay at home."

I went on to say that Abraham Lincoln was a great man because he knew how to laugh even when people made fun of him.

My story didn't work. Byrd and Larry had a crowd and they thought that they had to fight. They circled each other, each holding a straight blade in his right hand. I was ushered back from the action. During the fight, Larry slipped and fell. Byrd ran over to him, swinging his straight razor. I didn't think. I didn't plan on doing anything, but before I knew it I was bending over Larry. Byrd kept swinging his razor back and forth. He never meant to hurt me, but he swung and fell forward. I threw up my right arm, and the razor sliced my arm like a knife cutting butter. I was cut to the bone. Blood was everywhere. Larry cried. Byrd cried. I thought that I was going to bleed to death.

I was wrong. Thirty-three stitches later I awoke in a hospital emergency room, with adults and my peers filling the waiting rooms. I felt intense pain, but somehow I knew that my pain had been and would be what Dr. King called "redemptive suffering." Byrd and Larry were all right. I knew from that moment on that the "what" of my life had been answered; it was now just a matter of when. Even at a time of evil and evildoing, I knew that I was fortunate enough not to look at my friends sadly and shrug in helplessness.

The Mysterious Blood

In spite of knowing what I knew about the direction of my life, I still didn't have the tools I needed to be a preacher. I loved the ministry of Dr. King, but felt my destiny lay in a different direction. For the last months of my high school year, I felt the need to tell someone, "I'm going to be a preacher." But I did not.

But in June of 1965, everything changed. I was sitting in the kitchen, taking a lunch break, eating a grilled cheese sandwich and a glass of milk, and it came upon me suddenly. Sitting straight and tense, my eyes widened, as they sought to bore through what seemed to be a bright and blinding ray of light that engulfed me. My hands began to tremble, then my arms, then my entire body. I felt a great heat in my chest and blood begin to drip from my nose. A whisper came from all around me, and grew louder and louder, eventually shouting, "You must be about your father's business."

I began to cry, though I wasn't frightened. My Aunt Mary rushed into the kitchen, and ran for a towel for my nose. Uncle Curt, my younger sister Mary Ann, and my Aunt Inez followed, their eyes wide, as they watched my trembling body. When my Aunt Mary took the towel from my nose, there was no blood anywhere on it.

"I have to preach," I said, my voice somehow calm.

"I know," Aunt Mary replied.

I can't explain it, but I know that that experience became my compass. I knew why I was born and a portion of what I had to do. I had to publish the good news concerning a way of life that could be complete on all sides. Wherever I would have to go, whatever I would have to endure or do, this ambition would always be before me.

3

Preparation For Leadership

I MADE A public announcement to my church concerning my call to preach. Most were not surprised. A day was set for my "trial" sermon. I was informed that the church would determine if I had the "gift" to preach and license me accordingly. It was a long two weeks. Finally, the day arrived. Our church could only seat about two hundred people. People were not only standing in the aisles, they were gathered even in the parking lot. I was scared. Heaven was kind. But even on this special day I was hit with an issue that I would face in church after church, city after city, and circumstance after circumstance.

My pastor said, "Son, there are a lot of folks here and we are going to get some of that money." He then directed the ushers to take up three offerings. To this day I don't know what he or the church did with the money. I wanted to say something, but I knew that this was not the time and I was not the person. I had not even gotten my license. I was young. But even on the day of my inauguration into the ministry, I was being taught and shaped for the future. Money is a great servant, but it is a poor master, and I resolved on that day, even as I made my way to the sacred desk, that I would never permit money to become my ruler.

The Lord blessed the sermon. I had studied, but my efforts meant little until that same power that overwhelmed me on the day of my calling visited that sanctuary. It did. I have never been the same.

U.S. Air Force

As I began to view the church through the eyes of a future leader, I knew that I needed exposure beyond Alabama. I joined the Air Force. This was the first time in my life that I was placed in a living and prolonged work setting with white people. I was the product of a segregated Alabama. School, work, movies, and playgrounds were all segregated. I'd had only brief contact, and some of it made me glad that I didn't have to spend more time in a setting that was saturated with slurs and put-downs. I had been told that white people smelled like horses when they were wet. I could tell by the reception from some of the white troops from Mississippi that they, too, carried their own stories about how blacks smelled, wet and dry.

We were placed in Flight 933 at Lackland Air Force base in San Antonio, Texas. We were quickly informed that we all had something very important in common. We were "basics," and as such, we were told that we were the lowest thing in the whole world. We were lower than a snake's belly, according to our white drill sergeant. Our black drill sergeant added that he hated all basics, any color, size, or gender. This was my first experience with integration. It seemed to work. We soon became a group of equals—bonded by common needs, goals, threats, and hopes.

I soon learned, however, that there is a unity that lasts only as long as pressure is felt and circumstances warrant it. This unity comes through lack of options and lasts only as options remain elusive. It reminds me of a crisis that happened in a small Alabama town. Both whites and blacks were thrust into a narrow ravine due to flooding waters. The common threat of rising waters created a unity by necessity. They all drank water from a common bucket, but when help arrived and the hope of a rescue permeated the air, someone found a second bucket and placed it among the hopeful whites. A better option had to be found. Forced unity, I discovered, was no unity at all. Just an indefinite compromise.

This facade of unity would become a reality that I would be

compelled to identify and even employ on numerous occasions in future days. It was a good experience. The time would come when I would be forced to work with both white and black people that I knew I had better not trust.

From 3 A.M. early morning inspection to lights out at 9 P.M. the Air Force created a climate that demanded unity. Our only hope for the immediate reinforcer of liberty (nights out at the skating rink, movie passes, and weekend passes into the city of San Antonio) lay in the collective achievements of our entire flight. When one man failed we all failed. There was no black, white, or Latino failures. There was only United States Air Force Flight 933. We celebrated together and suffered together. The desire for liberty made each of us our brother's keeper.

Archie

I met some great people during my time in the Air Force, such as Archie. Archie was a white southern Baptist raised in Georgia. He was funny. At night when the lights were out he could talk like Donald Duck. Archie was a treat as much as dessert was in the mess hall. The official "lights-out" followed by the turning off of the barracks lights was often greeted by a Donald Duck monologue. Imagine a barrack of forty tired young men lying in the dark, when out of the darkness Donald Duck speaks, reading a "Dear John" letter. Archie certainly was a unique contribution to the morale of our flight. Archie also had some very X-rated disclosures about Daisy Duck that still cause me to blush even after thirty-five years. He was one of the first white people who I knew and called my friend.

Coronad

Coronad Johnson was a silky smooth brother from St. Louis, Missouri. Coronad's father had been a deacon in their church in Saint Louis. As we talked, I was amazed at the common characteristics. The black church, whether in St. Louis, Missouri or on Paul's Hill in Bessemer, Alabama, provided not only the hope of heaven for its people, but also the best hope for this earth. The need to be nurtured, spiritually fed, strengthened, focused, and empowered were all met in the church. The champion for justice, the hope for both a better life and life-style, and a voice assuring victory in an often hostile world thundered from the soul of the black church. Moral strength, civil rights, voter registration, civic pride, family values, cultural appreciation, positive self-esteem, compassion, and self-reliance are all gifts given by our church, regardless of denomination or location. The ministry of self-help seemed to evolve because our parents found out that the most that the governor and the governed can hope for is that laws will curb evil. They knew that laws would never cure it.

Even as I tell this story, I can recall the church stories we shared. The sixties enjoyed a massive social change for blacks because blacks honored their churches and the lessons that those churches taught. Even the most celebrated drunk in the community would try to straighten out his stagger when he walked by the holy ground of the church. At that time in history, comedians did not make fun of the church or its representatives, as is common today amongst many black comedians. Our young have had a serious decline in respect for the church because they have been taught it is something to laugh at and make fun of. You don't respect those you laugh at. It is disconcerting to see that the love of money has not only produced dangerous rap lessons on one hand, but it has also produced a prevalent sacrilege on the other.

Coronad and I shared stories about pretty girls in church and parental looks when you stepped out of line. Parents didn't have to say anything to you at church, they had this look, that told you to straighten up and get it together. We also discussed the Sunday morning sickness strategy. I would get too sick to go to church, but around 1 p.m., just in time to go to the Sunday movie matinee, I would experience a miracle. Of course, this strategy resulted in the "sick for church, sick all day" policy. It was remarkable that a child-rearing technique in Bessemer concerning churchgoing was also practiced in St. Louis. It was a time when parents had control of their children, which was to their children's benefit. It had nothing to do with size, but everything to do with moral authority.

Idaho

I cannot even recall his given or last name. He was white and stood about five feet eight. He was fascinated by air planes. More often than seldom Idaho messed up drill training sessions every time a plan flew over our heads. The "left, left, left, right, left" cadence call from our drill sergeant was broken by Idaho's upward look that led to "right, left, right" instead of "left, left, left, right, left." We lost two liberty opportunities and for young men aged eighteen through twenty, that was two too many. The white guys pulled several of us who were black over to the side during "chow time." They told us that we had to serve our country, save our flight, and ensure we got liberty by threatening to kill Idaho. They revealed that he had told them that he had never been around any Black people before and that he was afraid that they might "cut him." That stereotype didn't bother us at all. Duty called. Coronad made the threat. Idaho was healed of his airplane fantasy and we all left our dormitory singing "To the skating rink we go."

Bahamas Island Enlightenment

My first trip to the Bahamas provided me with far more than the beauty of white sandy beaches, picturesque sunsets, and exotically attractive plant and aquatic life. It introduced me to a custom that we as African-Americans had lost. A cursory view in the residential communities of Nassau revealed numerous unfinished houses. I wanted to know why.

My guide shared with me the ancient African custom of community building. While tourism is the first industry of the Bahamas and banking is the second, many locals choose to build as they are able to buy. In order to avoid a massive mortgage, the local inhabitants come together and help a homeowner build his or her house. They work as far as the money takes them. Twenty or so neighbors invest their time, energy, and expertise to help a fellow villager build. If the money runs out, they go home and return to complete the work according to an upturn in the financial resources of the homeowner. Sometimes it takes years, but the project comes into fruition as a result of corporate energy and goodwill.

This inspiring way of life arrested me. What one person could not do alone, several people could, and there were houses everywhere to prove it. This concept continues to be employed today. I wondered for many years why we as African-Americans did not and would not work with that same kind of impetus and cooperation. Through the years, this *"What we can do, we ought to do for ourselves"* attitude has found its way into the sermons I have preached, the lectures I have given, the books I have written, and organizations I have formed. Congregation after congregation has heard from me—we must stop expecting God and others to do for us that which we can do, but refuse to do for ourselves.

The Pastorate

While serving in the Air Force in Marquette, Michigan, I had my first experience in the pastorate. I helped establish a church and served as its pastor for almost a year. However, I guess that I cut my teeth at, of all places, my very own membership church, the New Saint Paul Baptist Church in Bessemer. I served there as pastor for two years. The challenge put me face to face with my deepest needs and most profound dreams. I led our church to become more involved in the daily needs and struggles of the parish.

At times, I picked up resistance and had no idea why. Sometimes you can find the center of something and have no idea what you've found. Sometimes you can fight a battle and have no idea who the real enemy is or the sheer and intimidating strength of your opposition.

I called for community meetings. I had not forgotten the men who had suffered with silicosis, nor those whose retirement hopes had been dashed to the grounds. An amazing thing happened. The word got out. There were more white miners present than black miners. I had to fight back my tears as I listened to the heartbreaking stories from heartbroken and sickly elderly men. We hired a lawyer, but the battle was long and costly. The lawyer dropped our case. Some said he sold us out. Somebody with a lot of money started spending it, and people stopped attending the meetings.

Some of the members in the church approached me. They said, "You are putting the church in danger."

My phone rang late one night. It was the voice of one of the elderly white miners. "Listen to me, he said. I got some things to tell you. You just might be the way God will change things for us common folk, but you won't be able to do it now. These folks got too much money. They can buy folks right in your church. Your own folks will turn against you. I can't help you 'cause I ain't got nothing to help with. Promise me you'll back off now, so you'll be able to fight another day."

I said, "I don't know what I'll do. Let me pray."

"Listen to me! The time will come when you will help a lot of folks, but right now you can't win. Your own will turn on you. Maybe you don't know it, but white folks always got some colored folks they use to keep folks like you from doing too much. I always knew it, but it never bothered me till now. The company lied to us. Their doctors lied to us. Lots of us are dying out. You can't stop that, but if you keep the good heart that you got, one day you'll help make things better."

A few weeks passed. I found out that he was right. That issue taught me a lot about the pain of limitation. It is painful when there is a discrepancy in goals between you and the folks you desire to help. A lovely elderly lady in my church sat me down and informed me of some of the things that the white miner had shared on a separate occasion.

It happened one sunny spring evening in late April, as civic and church activities bristled with burgeoning momentum across my already overcrowded schedule. Mrs. Gussie Wright, a thin ebony-skinned lady with large light brown eyes invited me to her modest, but meticulously kept home for some freshly baked tea cakes. Tea cakes were a southern delicacy, uncommonly made from freshly churned butter, milk, eggs, sugar, flour, and a precise amount of vanilla extract.

She greeted me at the door with a warm smile and asked to me to take a seat on a sofa that one of her daughters had told me was off limits for sitting, while she returned to the kitchen to fetch the tea cakes.

Sitting on that elegant ivory Queen Anne sofa gracefully surrounded by walls emblazoned with etchings of John and Robert Kennedy, Martin

Luther King, and George Washington Carver, I took a deep breath as the aroma of just-out-of-the-oven tea cakes permeated the air.

"I am so glad that you could come by today," she said as she returned with our treats and a pitcher of cold milk.

"Thanks for having me," I said and quickly took my first bite. As my teeth sank into the warm, soft, sweet, tender, yet firm crust, I hardly noticed the thick, well worn, tan-colored book that lay on the tray that held our treats.

"Pastor, I want to share something with you that I think will help you," she said as she picked up the book that read *Notes on the Alabama Constitution of 1901*. Mrs. Gussie had worked all of her adult life as a housekeeper, and for more years than she told any one of us, for a white judge who lived in Birmingham. Reaching into her eyeglass case, she withdrew her horn-rimmed glasses and with dainty circular motions, she cleaned them with a small white tissue. I had the feeling that she was about to tell me something important, so with a peaked curiosity, I leaned toward her and listened as she schooled me.

She explained that the Alabama constitution was drafted in 1901 to deal with "the Negro problem," and to keep all of the poor people (including whites) out of the political process where meaningful governmental decisions were made. The formation of the constitution was inspired by a group of conservative Democratic lawmakers known as the Bourbons. The Bourbons represented plantation operators and those who were connected with the various industries that were rising across the state at the dawning of the twentieth century. The Bourbons wrote restrictions on voting that ensured that only a few blacks and poor whites would be able to take part in political decision-making.

Most of the poor people who lived at that time were itinerant. They moved according to the availability of seasonal jobs. The constitution required a minimum of one year's residency in a county to be eligible to vote and ninety days of residency in a particular district.

The Bourbons also placed a dollar and a half per year poll tax. The tax was retroactive, which meant that a first-time voter, at any age, was charged one dollar and fifty cents per year, from twenty-one up to that person's age at the time of registration.

"Now," she asked rhetorically, "How many poor folks would be able to pay their poll tax if they voted for the first time when they were forty years old? I'll tell you not very many. Twenty-eight dollars and fifty cents was a lot of money back then."

"You're right," I said agreeably.

"I'm sure that most would not have been able to pay it. Along with literacy tests and disqualifying crimes such as stealing chickens, the 'haves' kept control over all the 'have nots.' It was about power and money then and it's about the same thing now. The Bourbons may have changed their name, but their descendants live on. The Ku Klux Klan are just stupid, poor, white people who have more in common with us than they have with the Bourbons. I'm telling you this because your fight for the miners is a battle with the Bourbons who still want to hold their power and make more money. Some of the people in our church are afraid. A few are just greedy, lazy, and satisfied to take handouts to keep us divided, scared, and confused. They will attack you and they will work to turn others against you."

I bowed my head in understanding. Then she fixed her eyes upon me and said, "God has work for you to do. Be strong and keep praying. I don't know where you will go, but I do know that you've outgrown us."

She was sincere and prophetic, as well as insightful, as she gave me names, dates, and even some of the arguments that the sell-outs would use to bring the work to a halt. Her prophetic words came to pass, but I knew in my heart that the day would come when I would once again confront these insidious foes of human aspiration and fair play.

Selma University

After four years of military duty in the Air Force, I began my formal theological education. Selma University in Selma, Alabama, was my mecca.

Owned by the Alabama Baptist State Convention (Black Baptists of Alabama), Selma University was an inspiring source of pride in the state of Alabama for Black Baptists from the steep hills of Huntsville in the north, to the sandy beaches of Mobile in the south. It stood in 1969 as a portrayal of human perseverance in the same city that had become infamous for what we labeled "Bloody Sunday."

"Bloody Sunday" took place on the Edmund Pettus Bridge in Selma. On that Sunday, in early March of 1965, I made the three-hour drive from Bessemer to Selma in order to march in support of voting rights for all Alabamians.

We were greeted at the bridge by state troopers who wielded clubs, whips, and iron pipes. Defenseless boys and girls, women (young and old), and unarmed men were beaten, battered, and tear-gassed unmercifully. We were taught, as young men in nonviolence training, to protect the children and women by covering them with our bodies.

I was afraid, but I covered a small girl. With my heart racing and my hands firm, I closed my eyes and thought that I was waiting to die. On that day I heard the unfiltered sounds of hate. It was an evil sound, vulgar and ominous. I heard the sounds of whips whistling through the air as they cut into the flesh of a person whose only crime was his or her desire to have the same respect that other people took for granted. I heard the pleas for mercy go unheeded and the cries for help ridiculed. I heard the language of the racist spoken in the volume and tone of pure loathing.

It seemed like an eternity as I lay stretched out, offering my backside, unshielded before dangerous horses and treacherous horsemen. Finally, I felt the comforting hands of one of the protest leaders on my shoulder as he told me to retreat back to the church.

My eyes burned from the fumes of the tear gas, but even with burning eyes, I could see a scene painted crimson with human blood. I saw one elderly black man stumble as he rapidly tore away his shirt to bandage a deep cut across his face that was bleeding profusely. There was an elderly lady, who someone called Mama Sister, limping and leaning on a young woman whose blouse had been ripped open. Two strong black men, with wounds of their own, picked up and carried a young white man who had been beaten so badly that he could not walk on his own.

As I looked at his bleeding and battered form, I surmised that this man had received the full brunt of the voices that had cried, "Nigger Lover! Nigger Lover!"

Tears and torture. Bleeding and broken. The face of evil. The sound of hate. A plethora of pain. It was indeed a "Bloody Sunday." But our suffering was not wasted. We gained the victory.

On March 21, 1965, Dr. Martin Luther King, Jr., under Secretary of the United Nations, Ralph Bunche and Reverend Ralph David Abernathy, led more than three thousand protestors in a second effort to march from Selma to Montgomery to gain voting rights for all Alabamians.

On March 25, 1965, I stood somewhere in the midst of twenty-five thousand black and white demonstrators as we joined hands in front of the state capitol building in Montgomery. Dr. King compared that event, in historical importance, to the march to the sea that was made by his hero of nonviolence, Mahatma Ghandi.

President Lyndon B. Johnson addressed a joint session of Congress after the "Bloody Sunday" scene in Selma. He titled his speech "We Shall Overcome." In that speech the president said:

> There is no Negro problem. There is no southern problem. There is no northern problem. There is only an American problem. A century has passed since the day of promise, and the promise is unkept. The time of justice has now come, and I can tell you that I believe sincerely, that no force can hold it back. It is right in the eyes of man and God that it should come, and *when it does, I think that day will brighten the lives of every American.*

In 1965, the Voting Rights Act was passed. I learned that sometimes the defeat experienced on one bad day can give birth to an ascendancy beyond your wildest dreams and plant the seeds for a future victory that many think can never be won.

Five years had passed since "Bloody Sunday." Changes had come. Selma University had stood and withstood the charges and the changes of the times. It was a symbol of what we, as African-American Baptists, could do with our prayers, finances, and influence.

Being an ordained black Baptist minister, I wanted desperately to prepare for the future. And I must also confess that when the school offered me a baseball scholarship, the thoughts of other school choices waned. My Aunt Mary was an alumnus of Selma University and she reviewed my choice with great favor.

Attending college as a minister, student athlete, and Air Force veteran, brought with it the perks that come with peer support. The ministers, athletes, and veterans each had both formal and informal networks into which I was fortunate enough to be warmly received. As I frequented the settings of ministers who spent a lot of time in the chapel, athletes who worked out in the gym, and veterans who gathered with regularity at Bertha's Coffee Shop, I took notice of two common faces in each arena.

Bobby Harris of Alabaster and Henry (Hank) Haskins of Demopolis were like myself—ministers, student athletes, and veterans. Bobby and Hank were Army vets. They teased me about the Air Force dress blue uniform, which they referred to as the uniform of a bus driver. I paid their ribbings no mind. However, I can recall a time or two in my lighter moments that I referred to the Army as my second choice if the Air Force had said no.

Bobby, brown-skinned, thinly built of average height and Hank, tall, dark, and muscular, soon became my two best friends and have remained so across the years. We played, prayed, and protested together as we completed our formal ministerial training.

Bobby styled as he scooped balls out of the dirt, as our first baseman. I batted lead-off, played short stop, and continued to spray hits with regularity to all parts of the field. Hank played right field, batted clean up, and in his own words, "Knocked the cover off the ball!" We were great friends.

In the holy precincts of the chapel, Bobby set the tone for preaching with his masterful sermon, "The Roads of Life," a sermon that stands to this day as a standard for my serious students of preaching to study. Hank, blessed with a rich baritone voice, thrilled our souls in ways that defy description as he would conclude his theologically mesmerizing messages with his own rendition of "Precious Lord take my hand." I studied, learned, and grew spiritually.

In the Old Testament the prophet Elisha had the seasoned wisdom of the prophet Elijah to guide him. In the New Testament the apostle Paul took special pride in having been a student of a doctor of the law whose name was Gamaliel. Bobby, Hank, and I were honored by heaven to join the grateful ranks of systematic theology students throughout Alabama and the nation who gratefully reflect upon the experience of having been students of Dr. Nathan Carter.

Dr. Carter, a man of average build whose piercing brown eyes often turned liquid with tears of gratitude as he taught us systematic theology, was both a Greek and Hebrew scholar and the closest example of all that a man of God should be that I've ever seen in my life.

When Dr. Carter spoke we beheld an instrument of two-way traffic with God. He taught us to humbly receive from God and to humbly give back to God as we served people and made their lives better. He now lives with God and his holy instructions continue to live among those who God developed through him. I pray that I can be half the teacher to my ministerial students that Dr. Carter was to us.

Leisure Time

I learned at an early age that you can't help anyone if you don't take good care of yourself. My tour in the Air Force afforded me the great luxury of falling in love with fishing. Regardless of whether it was a matter of hooking a twelve-pound Northern Pike in the icy waters of Labrador or crappie fishing in the southern waters of the mighty Alabama River in Camden, Alabama, I found priceless personal treasures as I navigated flowing water set off of rolling terrains at the edge of thickly planted trees.

Upon my discharge from the Air Force I purchased a simple fiberglass fourteen-foot Bass boat with a ten horsepower engine. My love of fishing made me a hit with my future wife and family. My brother-in-law Clarence Boswell, a native West Virginian, husband of Frankie, Essie

Ratcliffe, a homegrown Alabamian, husband of Rachel, and Hosea Hollingsworth, a native New Yorker, husband of Lizzie, all traded fish stories with me as the years raced by. I believe that we each lived by a code that said, "Never trust a fellow who won't eat at least one hush puppy."

Doe

For four straight days the mid-September weather had been perfect with sunshine and moderate daytime temperatures in the mid-seventies. The nights had been cool, but not chilly. It was unseasonably comfortable for the city of Selma, located in the heart of Alabama's black belt (so named because of the rich black soil) where temperatures often soared into the upper nineties even in the month of September.

As I ambled down the crosswalk that led from the chapel to the library at Selma University, thumbing through a book, I heard my name called by a familiar voice.

"Hey Horace, Horace Patterson. Is that you? Got a minute?"

I raised my head and wheeled in the direction of the voice that summoned me. It was Charles Manzie, standing six feet tall, dressed in a navy blue blazer, wearing a white shirt, red tie, and white trousers. Charles had been a high school classmate of mine at Wenonah High School. Unbeknownst to me, he had also acknowledged his call into the ministry after spending four years in Detroit, Michigan.

We had lost touch with each other and neither one of us knew that the other was enrolled at Selma University.

Standing proudly in the student parking lot, Charles was surrounded by four of his well-dressed classmates, as they admired his new ebony teal Pontiac Grand Prix. He beckoned me over. I felt a bit uneasy. I had just come from a bit of chapel quiet time, dressed in a pair of faded sweat pants and a T-shirt. I made my way toward him. We greeted each other and in spite of my reluctance, Charles, with his widening smile and warm good nature, hugged me.

"Man, what are you doing here?" he asked.

"In school. How are you?" I replied.

"We've got to get together and talk."

"Right. I'll look forward to it."

Then he turned to his classmates and said, "Folks forgive me for my bad manners. This is Horace Patterson. He used to be known as Mr. Baseball in our hometown. He is also the pastor of his membership church in Bessemer. The Lord said, 'A prophet is without honor in his own country.' Horace Patterson is one of those fellows who had the nerve to do what most of us preachers dare not do."

He shook his head teasingly but admirably, and said, "I'll bet it's no picnic pastoring people who knew you as a baby."

I laughed and shook hands with his classmates, Willie Askew from Mobile, Daisy Marshall from Monroe County, Eddie Marshall from Monroeville, and David Steele from Chicago, Illinois.

They were all dressed attractively, having come from some community meeting where they had made formal presentations on the ways in which the university and community could work together. They called it a "Town and Gown" meeting. Being conscious of my sweats in the presence of those who were so attractively attired, I sought to end the conversation and retreat to my apartment off campus, but Willie Askew insisted on conversing with me. With eager eyes and rapid speech, he said, "I heard your sermon in chapel last week and I still remember your subject. It was 'Sometimes God Upsets to Set Up.' Right?"

I said, "Yes, you're right," and as I spoke, I found myself fumbling for words, partly in order to be courteous, and partly so that I could hide my embarrassing preoccupation with the petite lovely figure that approached us.

Weighing no more than a hundred pounds, she stood about five feet tall, attired in an immaculate yellow suit highlighted with gold buttons. Around her neck she wore a single strand of pearls. Her smooth, heart shaped face, the shade of soft beige, seemed to glow as she smiled. Her long, thick, silky hair bounced beneath her shoulders as she walked toward us, and the background of the afternoon sun billowed against a sky of serene and spotless blue behind her.

Willie Askew read the seized look that donned my face in spite of my verbal camouflage and asked, "Would you like to meet her?"

"Yes, I would. But I'm not very presentable at this point," I said, while secretly scolding myself for not having put on something better looking than a pair of sweats and a T-shirt. I had plenty of clothing. I had special ordered five tailor made silk suits from Japan before I finished my military duty. I had turtle neck shirts, dress shirts, flare leg pants, and there I was dressed in faded sweats and a T-shirt.

Sensing my discomfort, Charles said, "Don't worry about that. You look fine."

Willie Askew replied, "To tell you the truth, I think she was impressed with your chapel sermon last week."

Daisy Marshal honed in saying, "She's my home girl. She won't judge you by what you're wearing and besides, if you walked out now it would seem rude and you don't want her to think you are rude, do you?"

"Of course not," I replied, somewhat sheepishly.

I waited as she arrived. We were introduced. Her name was Dolia McIntosh. As I scanned her beautiful face closely, I received, as what I defined, a curious glance in return. She politely returned my greeting with a pleasing, "Hello. I am very happy to meet you."

Her voice had a flirting sweetness to it, as we engaged in telling each other where we were from, while being keenly aware of the audience around us. Speaking with a confidence that I did not feel, I assured her that we would chat at another time. Whatever feelings her eyes contained were hidden, as she turned her head to answer the group's question about going to Pizza Hut as they had planned. They asked me if I wanted to join them. I said, "Thanks, but no. Maybe another time."

Before leaving, I cast a final look into the eyes of Dolia and hoped that the disappointment that I read was only because I did not accompany her to Pizza Hut.

It was a Thursday afternoon. I had to leave Selma each Friday in order to return to Bessemer for the weekend so that I could assume my priestly duties as a pastor. Sick visitation, some counseling, teaching a bible study class on Saturday night, and preaching during the 11 a.m. worship hour provided me with a rich menu for the weekend.

As I prepared for my weekend, I found myself overwhelmed with thoughts of this beautiful, sweet spirited, and regal-looking young woman by the name of Dolia McIntosh. Yet I was almost afraid to hope, for fear of disappointment, that she was thinking of me as I thought of her. My mind replayed every word she spoke and froze every look that she turned my way.

I arose early that Friday morning, hosed off my 1968 powder blue Buick duce and a quarter (225 Electra), showered, dressed in my best silk suit, and drove to the campus of Selma University. I stood at my car pretending to read, but almost desperately searching for the sight of Dolia. She had mentioned that she had morning classes in the Denkins building, so I parked in front of it and waited.

She arrived at 7:30 a.m. I did not waste any time. I walked up to her and said, "Good morning."

With a heart-penetrating smile, she raised her eyebrows in surprise and returned my greeting. "Good morning. This is a pleasant surprise. How are you?"

"Fine thanks. How was your pizza?"

"It was great. We really did have a good time. You should have come along," she said. Her voice tone was far softer and sweeter than I had remembered from our brief exchange on the day before.

Dressed in a stunning lime green dress, she seemed to complement the crisp and fresh ascension of the morning sunrise. Her smooth high-cheek bones, dancing brown eyes, and the way she tossed her thick silky brown hair about as we chatted set me at ease in one sense but also intimidated me in a way that I had not known before. The scent of her perfume. The beauty of gleaming innocence. The emanating glow of tenderness. The apparent presence of unpretentiousness. The elegance of simplicity. The residence of compassion. I don't know whether it was her gleaming facial features, her long silky hair, her penetrating smile, her soft-toned voice, or the sum total of them all that made her so enchanting and remarkable to me.

"I have to go to Bessemer for the weekend to attend to my church duties. I'll be leaving this afternoon. May I have your telephone number? I'd really like to get to know you better if it's all right. I mean, unless you're married or engaged or something?"

With a sly grin she replied, "Well, I am not married and I am not engaged. Are you?"

"Of course not."

Then she opened a blue notebook, scribbled down her phone number and said, "Be careful driving home. Maybe we'll have a chance to talk when you get back." With those words she walked away, heading for her 8 a.m. Biology lab class. I watched her as she walked away and patted myself on the back because as awkward as I felt, I had not made a complete fool out of myself.

Tethered to thoughts of Dolia, my weekend raced by. In my heart I knew that what I felt for her was not some enchantment that would pass. When I returned to Selma, I called her and asked if she would like to take in a movie. In her bubbly voice she said, "A movie would be nice. What movie do you have in mind?"

I replied, "Doe. May I call you Doe?"

"Nobody has ever called me Doe, and to be shamefully honest, I kind of like it, especially the way you say it. I hope that's not being too forward."

"You could never be too forward. I'll be honest with you, it doesn't matter what kind of movie we see. I just want to be with you."

We went to a drive-in and talked through the movie. I was engulfed in a wave of feelings that swept the world away.

We spent some time together each and every day that I was in Selma. Soon our days turned to weeks and the weeks hastened the fall semester to an end. The more I learned about Doe, the more deeply I fell in love with her. We spent evenings sitting on blankets watching sunsets and we talked about everything from our life goals to our most embarrassing moments.

Chapel at Selma University was mandatory. I had missed my morning classes. I had eaten something that had made me miserable. I had been up all night. When I finally awoke on that Tuesday morning in January of 1970, Doe stood over my bed. She had heard that I was sick and came by to nurse me back to the land of the living. In thirty minutes

I was up. My roommates renamed me Lazarus. She had raised me up and done it in time for me to make chapel.

Raising me up seems to have been a theme in Doe's life. Especially when I've been most vulnerable. My story is her story finally told. As an educator for twenty-five years, she has lived out her dream to inspire and motivate children. As a teacher, she always felt that it was her responsibility to create a climate that allowed each child to be successful. As a public school principal, she has always viewed her role as that of an instructional leader. Her unique ability to create a nurturing environment has yielded both public and private dividends.

On June 13, 1970, six months after my "Lazarus" experience, Doe and I were married. Neither one of us knew that our odyssey together would reach a state where an entire city's future would be shaped by our response to adversity.

As the mother of our three wonderful children, Horace Jr., Jay, and Ivy Eleece, Doe remains our heroine and our heart.

Marion County

From the fall of 1971 to June of 1974, I served as pastor of the Liberty Baptist Church in Alabaster, Alabama. It was while I served that congregation that I became more convinced that the black church had to lead the way for every kind of decent change that was needed. People change for several reasons. They change when they get a chance to, they change when they realize that they can, and they change when it hurts too much to stay the same.

Stories of red-lining, employment discrimination, judicial apathy and injustice, and police brutality all pointed to our community's need to become stronger, educationally, spiritually, politically, and economically. Just as Christ could not turn a deaf ear to the pious hypocrisy of pseudo-priests and the unnecessary submissive language of self-inflicted victims, I found myself becoming more and more combative with both the historical evils from the outside and the strange emerging apathy from the inside. It was not enough to preach about Jewish unity, the Italians' sense of family, Korean industry, or the Bahamians' practice of neighbors helping neighbors build and rebuild. With every sermon that I preached and with every heartbreaking story that I listened to, I felt a more profound call to make things happen.

Ozzie Huff, a former teacher at Selma University, called. Doe took the call while I was not home. He needed help—he was running for sheriff of Marion County. Many of the whites were threatening blacks; some even dared them to vote for Huff. Although I was not home, Doe knew that I would try to help. She relayed the message. I went to Marion County and met with leaders of their community. There were even a couple of whites who knew that a change was needed. They also knew that it was dangerous, and stayed in the background. At times I angrily challenged the ministers and church leaders by asking, "Why should white people help you, when you won't help yourselves?"

Ozzie lost the race. On the day of the election, I became a target, and my friends had to lock me in the trunk of a car and sneak me out of town. Some of the blacks, who resented me, had fingered me. Some who appreciated me had militantly misrepresented me.

In the latter case, I was like the ancient Chinese monarch who met one of his shoguns and asked him where he was coming from. The shogun replied, "I am coming from the east, where I have been killing your enemies."

The monarch said, "But I have no enemies in the east."

The warrior thought about all of the blood that he had spilled in the name of his king and said, "Your Excellency, maybe you had no enemies in the east before I went there, but since I have made wives into widows and sons into orphans in your name, take my word, trust me, you now have enemies in the east."

I learned on that day in Marion County that sometimes well-meaning, enthusiastic people can say, do, and react to issues that can create havoc and grave danger for you by what they say and do in your name. I also remembered the insight given to me by a dying white miner.

I remembered his warning as he told me that there were power brokers who would and could pay certain black folks to create division and destroy unity. I remembered Mrs. Gussie Wright's lecture to me about the Bourbons and how they thrived by keeping blacks and poor whites in the economic and political back seats.

I also learned a great deal about Doe and the remarkable strength that this beautiful woman possessed. I did not tell her about the dangers that I had encountered because I did not want to worry her, but she found out. One of the community leaders had called from Marion the day after the election to make sure that I had arrived home safely and had also recounted for her the election day events with special emphasis on having had to sneak me out of town in the trunk of a car.

When I arrived home that night, Doe greeted me warmly and held me so closely that I could feel her entire petite, but trembling body, shaking in my embrace.

"We have to talk. Today I found out that those people in Marion County had to sneak you out of town," she said in that soft voice tone that is peculiar to her alone. As she spoke, I saw tears that spoke of her disappointment in me well up in those beautiful brown eyes. It was the first time she had cried in front of me.

"Honey," she said, "I love you more that I can ever explain in word or deed. I need to know about the bad times and bad things that happen in your life, as well as the good times and the good things. Please don't close me out or try to protect me as if I am some kind of fragile figurine. I am not."

I sat down on the sofa motionless, embarrassed by my foolish male chauvinism and chagrined by my obvious lack of sensitivity.

Doe and I sat there that night, with the light from a solitary lamp and talked until the early morning hours. I did not mean to be macho or selfish. I had done what I had been doing all my life with my hurt and my fears. I had kept them to myself. It was good to share them with someone who loved me enough not to abandon me because of them.

Dexter Avenue Baptist Church

During my junior year at Selma University, I preached a sermon in chapel titled "Traveling Through the Valley of Baca." My subject was taken from the eighty-fourth number of Psalms. Relying upon historical data and maps that questioned whether a literal valley of Baca existed, I laid emphasis upon the spiritual reality.

My thesis portrayed a valley of Baca in every life by defining it as a hot, dry, lonely, and intimidating stretch through which Biblical worshipers had to pass in order to experience the joys of Temple worship. "While the valley of Baca might not be found on a map of ancient Israel," I asserted, "it is referred to in the Bible. And it is in the Bible because it is a difficult place in every life through which we must pass."

The redemptive value of the Biblical narrative pointed out that there were some special people who traveled through that mysterious valley. They turned it into a well by digging into the dry earth and planting vessels that could hold water during the rainy seasons. Those who planted the vessels became blessings to those who trekked the inevitable canyon behind them. My challenge was a call to use pains and experiences as instruments of blessings for others.

Dr. A. W. Wilson, president of the Alabama Baptist State Convention was present in that chapel service. Dr. Wilson, an elderly pastor and a man of great influence pulled me to the side and asked to chat with me before returning to his home in Montgomery, Alabama.

"Reverend Patterson, I have been asked by Dexter Avenue Baptist Church to recommend to them a pastor. You don't have to make any decisions, but I would like for you to preach for them in a worship service. If you preach there, I know that there will be some who will want you as pastor," he said somewhat smiling as if he knew something about me that I did not know about myself.

"Thank you for your kind support. I am presently pastoring a wonderful congregation, but I will be happy to preach at Dexter," I said.

"Good. I'll give your name, address, and phone number to the church officer that contacted me."

I was deeply honored to have been thought of so well by Dr. Wilson.

Within a week I received a phone call from the pulpit committee and scheduled a Sunday for preaching.

Dexter Avenue Baptist Church in Montgomery, Alabama was, to me, a great church. It had been pastored by both Dr. Vernon Johns and

Dr. Martin Luther King, Jr. I was deeply humbled.

As I stood and preached behind the sacred desk where great men had served, I stood in awe of a God who could direct the steps of a young man from Paul's Hill in Bessemer to a station of historical significance.

Doe and I really enjoyed meeting that congregation. The people were kind and complimentary. As Dr. Wilson had predicted, the church officers asked to include my name as a candidate for the pastorate, and I was asked to preach a second sermon. I met with the church officers. They were sincere and gifted men, but Dexter was not to be the place of my calling. However, each experience that I underwent would prepare me for a role that I could never in my wildest dreams anticipate.

4

Talladega, Alabama

P RIOR TO THE spring of 1974, I had never been to Talladega, Alabama. I had lived less than one hundred miles away most of my life, yet I had never been to this city of nineteen thousand people. It is strange, because Talladega College was legendary at Wenonah High School in Birmingham. During the early sixties, you had to be at least a B+ student to even be considered for admission, or so we were told.

Things were going great. I had resigned from the New St. Paul Church to accept a larger congregation at the Liberty Baptist Church in Alabaster, Alabama. I had also returned to my hometown of Bessemer. Doe had given birth to our first child, Horace Jr., and she was about to graduate cum laude from Miles College. I was in a building program at the church and we were becoming, as a church family, more involved in the process of being a part of the solution. We did this by developing food and clothing banks, organizing job fairs, financial counseling, ongoing voter registration, and participation programs.

The phone rang and a man by the name of George Peasant was on the other end. Mr. Peasant introduced himself to me as the chairman of the deacon board at the historic Mount Canaan Baptist Church in Talladega. I knew of the church because of my church history studies as a theological student. I also knew of the church's deep historical contributions. It was founded by Dr. William McApine, who was the great-grandfather of Eunice Johnson of *Ebony* magazine. Dr. McApine had been one of the founders of my beloved Selma University and had served as its president. As Mr. Peasant spoke, my mind raced as I recounted the history of that church's famous pastor. He had been a contemporary and good friend of Dr. Booker T. Washington of Tuskegee University. "Reverend Patterson," he said, "we need a pastor with your kind of vision and commitment. I have spoken with people in your hometown who have known you for many years. I have also spoken with ministers across the state, including one of our previous pastors, Reverend Herman Spruill. You have come to us highly recommended. Will you come, at your convenience, one Sunday and preach in our worship service?"

"Mr. Peasant, I am a civil rights activist. I don't know if your congregation would be a match for me. I know that your church has a rich history, but I am not familiar with your position on the recent issues that confront our people." I spoke directly to the issue of community activism because I had reached a stage where I knew that some churches frowned upon their pastors' involvement in community and civil affairs. These kind of churches were, in the words of Dr. D. L. Moody, "So heavenly minded that they were no earthly good." In my heart I knew that I could never be happy in a church setting where people simply came together for a good time and left the world in which they lived unaffected.

"I believe that you will find our congregation to be very enlightened and responsive to a leader with your passion."

"I'll be happy to come and preach to you. Thanks for the invitation."

We scheduled a Sunday for my visit. After I hung up the phone Doe asked, "What was that all about?"

"The Mount Canaan Baptist Church in Talladega has asked me to preach for them. I have agreed. They seem to have a real need for leadership. I don't know why but I feel like I might be able to be of some help by preaching to them."

Doe said, "Okay. I've never been . . ." Horace Jr. cried out before she could finish her sentence. He was only eight months old. He was the perfect baby with a head full of the most curly black hair and his mother's high cheek bones. It was feeding time and that was a task that so engulfed us that the thoughts of Talladega waned for the moment.

Doe, Horace Jr., and I traveled to Talladega two weeks after my conversation with Mr. Peasant. We were greeted by a warm congregation. A lovely lady by the name of Bettye Kirsey invited us to her home for dinner. She was a bronze-skinned, middle-aged, elementary school teacher who was serving as a member of the pulpit committee. "Well Reverend Patterson, please tell me what you think of us," she said as she filled the formal lace-covered dining table with fried chicken, mashed potatoes, collard greens, okra, field peas, corn on the cob, crackling cornbread, and sweet potato pie for dessert.

"I'm very happy to meet you and I think that you have a very kindhearted congregation," I replied hoping that she would not press me for an assessment that I was not prepared to render. She didn't.

Her lovely soft spoken daughter Carolyn, a girl in her teenage years, seemed mesmerized by Horace Jr. and it appeared that he was enjoying the attention cast upon him by his new-found admirer.

The meal was wonderful. The conversation was enjoyable and rather lighthearted at times when Bettye spoke of her many relatives who had enjoyed a long history as members of Mt. Canaan.

After dinner we returned to our home in Bessemer, grateful for the experience, but maybe even more appreciative for the life that we had and the future that we anticipated by remaining where we were.

A couple of weeks had passed and I received another call from Talladega. This time the voice identified himself as William Cokely, secretary to the board of deacons. Mr. Cokely invited me to a meeting with the deacon board. He informed me that the church wanted me to serve as its pastor. At that time the idea was not very attractive to me; I had done my research. The church was founded in 1870, but its roots went back to the Good Hope (white southern Baptists) Church. African-Americans worshiped and were seated in the balcony of the white church as late as 1929. The official black congregation became a separate congregation within the walls of the white church, and according to church minutes in August of 1869, a resolution was adopted by the Good Hope Baptist Church:

"Resolved, that in as much as there is too much conflict for two separate congregations to worship in the same building, it is proper to revoke the agreement heretofore made with the colored people granting them use of the church building for a weekly prayer meeting. Resolved further, that we the white members of this church agree to aid the colored people in the erection of a suitable house of worship for themselves." August term minutes—1869.

The history raised a lot of questions for me. If the resolution was revoked in 1870, then why did blacks voluntarily settle for seats in the balcony as late as 1929? Why did the church have such a long list of pastors? From 1870 to 1974 there had been twenty-four pastors. In one hundred and four years the church had had twenty-four pastors, which was an average of four years and three months per pastor. I was lukewarm to the idea of meeting with the leadership, but I consented. We met, and they impressed me as good, decent, committed men.

One man by the name of Walter Baker, Sr. questioned me intensely about my belief system concerning the role of the church. "I've been in this town a long time," he said. "We need a pastor real bad and this town needs a leader who will have the brains and guts to help us all."

Mr. Baker's sentiments were expressed by several others. I questioned them concerning their support. The clear majority spoke in the affirmative. I told them that I would give them an answer within a week. I was impressed, but as I said, things were going great for me. I drove home. I told Doe about the meeting and informed her that I didn't want to go to Talladega. She smiled and said, "Okay."

I went to bed, and I awoke in a sweat. I'd dreamed that our home was on fire. I collected myself and went back to sleep. I awoke again, this time with tears in my eyes. It was 3 a.m. I'd dreamed my house had burned and my baby had died and a voice above my head spoke, saying, "The Lord gives and the Lord takes away." This time I got the message. I repented for my arrogance. I fell on my knees. My fears lost some of their nightmarish grip and my sleep was no longer troubled. I could have called Mr. Cokely at the same hour. I had been telling the Lord what I had in Bessemer. He reminded me that I had nothing, anywhere, without him. I repented and we were Talladega-bound.

A City of Great Wonders

I made every effort that I could to understand the city of Talladega. I often found myself enchanted by its history and overwhelmed by the stately beauty of its dogwood trees, dazzling splendor of blooming azaleas, and the mesmerizing charm of its old antebellum homes and buildings. A city rich in historic preservation, Talladega pointed proudly to its past.

My research informed me that the Battle of Talladega was fought on November 9, 1813. Selocta, the son of Chief Cinnabee of the Creek nation, volunteered to make his way through hostile lines in order to reach General Andrew Jackson so that the town would be saved from a large force of hostile warriors. The rich land, beautiful clean streams and excellent climate caused many of the men in Jackson's army to settle in what was called at that time the beautiful valley of Talladega.

A final treaty with the Creek nation was signed on March 24, 1832, and although there still remained a dispute over the method of settlement, Indian domination of the area ended.

I took a walk along South Street to visit Talladega's Silk Stocking district. It is an L-shaped area of approximately one-hundred and thirteen acres and is a treasure trove of magnificent homes dating from 1833 to the early 1990s. The structures range from simple, unadorned cottages to elaborate Queen Anne and Eastlake houses. Turrets, shingles, turned ornaments, decorative chimneys, and stained glass are abundant.

A majority of the homes in this district were built between 1885 and 1915 for leading merchants, lawyers, doctors, and city officials, and consequently were the finest in town. The wives of these men of wealth could have afforded to wear silk stockings, thus, the name Silk Stocking district.

I was quite fortunate to be able to enroll as a student at Talladega College and graduate with a major in clinical psychology and a minor in history. As I walked the hallowed and manicured grounds of Talladega College, I soon discovered that there are some things you can't fully explain. You just have to experience them for yourself. Talladega College is nationally known for academic excellence, but the spirit of Talladega College shares a special touch with those who embrace it.

On November 20, 1867, Talladega College became a seed planted in the minds of William Savery and Thomas Tarrant, both former slaves. On that day the people of the Talladega Community of Freedom decided that the education of their black youth was the key to the preservation and growth of their recently granted freedoms. Savery Library, to this day, houses the historically significant Amistad murals by Hale Woodruff, depicting the successful quest for freedom by captured Africans aboard the slave ship *The Amistad*.

I further discovered that the Alabama Institute for Deaf and Blind called Talladega its home. The Institute was founded as the Alabama School for the Deaf in 1858 by Dr. Joseph Henry Johnson. With him came his wife and thirteen-year-old brother Seaborn, who enrolled as the school's first student on October 4, 1858.

Dr. Johnson's first steward, Reuben Asbury, left to fight in the Civil War. He returned to Talladega in 1864 almost totally blind. Through his ideas and determination, the Alabama School for the Blind was founded on ASD's campus in 1867.

The Alabama Institute for Deaf and Blind has regional centers across the state of Alabama. It is the foremost international institution for services to blind and deaf persons from birth to elder years and it continues, to this day, to call the city of Talladega its home.

As I visited the library, Chamber of Commerce, and listened as people enthusiastically enlightened me, I found a special fondness growing in my heart for Talladega. The fondness of which I speak was not geared simply to what I read and was told about Talladega, but for what I saw.

I was invited to the Presbyterian Home for Children. A home that was born as a child of necessity during the war between the states. Its purpose then was to serve the homeless children of families ravaged by the war, fought by brother against brother.

As I toured the massive buildings that stood in my time to serve children ravaged by another war, a war with poverty, illness, abandonment, and abuse, a war in which children are caught in the middle of separation and mobility, I found a fondness for Talladega welling up in my very soul.

The Talladega Superspeedway, marketed as the world's fastest track, the International Motor Sports Hall of Fame, the sight of a blind rehabilitation teacher from the Alabama Institute for Deaf and Blind patiently and professionally teaching a blind person ways to safely navigate the streets of the city, the look of a child who might have lost his or her way, but safely coping in the Presbyterian Home, and the loving people that I met endeared this city of wonders to my heart.

As I looked at the city for what it was I also wondered what it might become if it could find the heart to deal with its threats and build upon its obvious assets.

The Twenty-Four Horsemen

Mount Canaan Baptist Church is located on West Battle Street, which is State Highway 21 and is a main thoroughfare. In 1974, located less than fifty feet from the church on the same side of the highway, was a nightspot called the Twenty-Four Horsemen. I quickly discovered that Sunday night appearances were extremely deceptive. The church parking lot was filled with cars not from the Sunday night worshippers, but from the Sunday night partygoers. Monday mornings often revealed the aftermath debris: liquor bottles, beer cans, and other items that even the town drunk would find embarrassing in the presence of a church.

It did not take me very long to create some enemies who would spend a good deal of time and money in efforts to destroy my influence. In the city of Talladega it was against the norm to sell or distribute alcoholic beverages fifty feet from a church. This was, at that time, generally the rule in the Bible Belt. However, this disconcerting reality never elicited the ire or the intervention of local law enforcement. It was a "black thing," as one of the police representatives reminded me. I thought to myself that if this is a "black thing," it's a sorry "black thing" that needs to go the way of the dinosaur. Some places ought to be too holy for beer cans and liquor bottles. The House of God is such a place.

I preached, prayed, talked, and worked along with a group of faithfuls from Mt. Canaan and eventually, the nightspot closed down. A while later, I was approached by an individual who offered me 500 dollars a month if I would only be quiet. He had plans to reopen the nightspot and turn it into an overnight cat house. When I told him what he could do with his 500 dollars a month, he said, "God damn you Preacher. You won't last another year in this town. We will destroy you. Your name will be mud and we know just how to make it mud."

There was a part of me that recoiled at the vulgar scene. I stood there, amazed at the routes some people can trek, the depths to which, pulled down by an evil force stronger than themselves, they can fall.

I knew that this issue was not simply about money. It was about moral authority. I said, "Do what you think is right." I knew that this guy and his cohorts would deal me some discomfort, but I've always felt that "pain is inevitable, but misery is a choice." Whether it has been a matter of spreading filthy rumors, finding weak members in the church to become oppositional, or recruiting candidates to run against me in public office, my enemies have been consistent.

Those few antagonists who are black have sought to fulfill their prophecy even though twenty years have passed. I relay this account because it is probably not unique in Talladega. Sometimes the people who steal our moral strength to be and to do what must come to pass are those who seem to be like us in every way, except heart. Dr. Warren Wiersbe is correct when he says, "The problem of the heart is always the heart of the problem."

Growth Within

The church responded to leadership. The deacons kept their word. They responded as we organized the church with a host of programs including tutorials, drug education, benevolence, senior services, counseling, enrichment, and spiritual deepening among others. The detractors without did not halt the progress within. We began long-range planning. Our goals included more than 1.5 million dollars in church renovations, buildings, and property acquisitions. I knew that this would mean that at some point I would have to become a bivocational pastor. It was a choice that I was prepared to make. I was convinced that this city could become my home. "Things turn out best for people who make the best of the way things turn out" has been more than a motto, but a motivation for me in many ways.

As I sat in my office in the church one evening in late October of 1975, as autumn ushered in the multicolored foliage of the season, I was startled by a rapid knock upon the door. It was the chairman of my deacon board Eddie Player, who was beaming with enthusiasm.

He was smiling, to a degree even above his normal bubbling personality. A man of average height with dark brown eyes, he always seemed to possess the mannerisms of one of those rare people who never meet a stranger.

"Reverend Patterson, I just wanted to tell you that the budget committee says that we have more than doubled our income compared to last year's figures."

"That's great news isn't it?" I replied.

"It's not just great news, it's a miracle," he said as he sat down thumbing through the newly compiled financial report.

We chatted for a while and he left but not before leaving me a copy of the report that had generated the cause of his celebration.

As I browsed through the report I did feel a sense of gratification until I reached the section that was labeled as Gifts From Friends. There it was. I couldn't believe it, but there in bold print was the name of the man who had vowed to destroy me. He had given a gift of 100 dollars to the church. My thoughts raced. Blood flushed my face as I sat there with startled eyes.

"What's this all about?" I asked myself, convinced that regardless of whatever he had given, he was definitely not a friend of our church. The more I thought about his gesture the more convinced I was that this character just might be trying to buy some influence in the church. I wrestled with my lower self and briefly entertained some foolish thoughts such as telling my board of deacons about my encounter and asking them to return the money. But as I battled between my thoughts, I searched my own heart and from that search I began to ask myself if what I was feeling was true righteous indignation for the glory of God or plain old revenge from a man who had been cursed and who had not really forgiven the man who had cursed him.

I opened my Bible and the verse that my eyes fell upon was Psalm 76 verse 10 which reads, "Surely the wrath of man shall praise thee." As I read that verse I was reminded that God is able to make the anger and even the evil of people praise him. I recalled a story I once heard about a minister who was leading a religious service. A drunken man threw a well-aimed potato that found its mark on the face of the minister. The minister was momentarily sidetracked, but regained composure and finished the service. After the service concluded, the minister prayed with the potato in his hand and a voice seemed to say, "Plant it." The minister obeyed. The potato was planted and a whole basket of potatoes was harvested from a potato thrown with unkind motives. The message to me was too obvious for argument. If God could use that potato then he could also use the 100 dollars. I prayed with that finished report in my hand and referred the matter to wiser hands than mine.

Wednesday, November 24, 1976

I had started a process that would eventually land me in two seats of conflict. On August 31, 1976, the House of Representative, District 55 seat became vacant. The former representative, Mr. John Teague of Childersburg, vacated the seat as he was elected to the State Senate District 19 seat in a special election. Mr. Quinten Gresham, a social work professor, Dr. Bernard Bray, a political science professor—both employed at Talladega College at the time—Dr. Thomas Y. Lawrence, assistant superintendent of Talladega city schools, and the church treasurer of Mt. Canaan approached me. They pointed out the uniqueness of the times and asked me to run for the vacant legislative seat.

I did not give an immediate answer. I had to talk with Doe and the Lord, but not necessarily in that order. I also spoke with several community leaders, including other ministers, civic leaders, and senior church members, church mothers like Mrs. Sara Cobb and Mrs. Julia Thomas. They all concurred, citing that it was an off-season for elections, that this would be a special election and not many people would vote, meaning that I stood a chance if I could get my voters to the polls, and Mrs. Cobb reminded me that it was a matter of me practicing what I had been preaching to them for two years. It was time to get involved, beyond the walls, in a way that could impact asphalt streets before my people walked on streets of gold. Mrs. Thomas reminded me of that wonderful motto shared with us by Mrs. Eula Cokely, a deaconess in our church, from the Christophers: "It is better to light one candle than to curse the darkness."

Mr. Walter Baker, Sr. heard about it and asked to see me. He spoke with passion ringing in his voice, "This is why we wanted you to come here. This is what we have been praying for. You got to do it no matter whether you win or lose. We will all win because it will show all these people that we've got a leader that we chose, not some 'house nigger' that they left in charge of the plantation." He went on to re-preach a sermon to me that I had preached to them entitled "A Time For Involvement."

I remembered the message and had introduced it by saying that, "Uninvolvement always precedes danger." Quoting Edmund Burke, I'd passionately said, "All that remains for evil to triumph is for good people to do nothing." I had told the story of Martin Niemoller, the courageous German pastor who suffered years of imprisonment for his opposition to the Hitler regime.

Mr. Baker had committed Niemoller's words to memory. "We have failed, for we knew the wrong and the right path, but we did not warn the people and allowed them to rush forward to their doom. In Germany, they came first for the Communist, and I didn't speak up because I wasn't a Communist. Then they came for the Jews, and I didn't speak up because I wasn't a Jew. Then they came for the trade unionist, and I didn't speak up because I wasn't a trade unionist. Then they came for the Catholics, and I didn't speak up because I was a Protestant. Then by the time they came for me, there was no one left to speak up."

I smiled and said, "Amen." His memory was better than mine, and I'd been the one who had preached the sermon.

It was a Democratic primary. Six candidates qualified. I was the only black. One white voter that I approached was just angry that a black man had the nerve to run for the legislative seat. He looked at me and said angrily, "All I can say is that I'm glad my daddy ain't alive to see this." He then took my card and threw it to the ground and stepped on it.

I persevered, and the day of the election, to the surprise of many, I led the field with 934 votes. The closest candidate to me was Wallace Shoemaker, a self-employed pharmacist from Childersburg. I did not have 50 percent plus one vote, so a run-off was set for December 14, 1976. I anticipated the historical response to at-large elections in the South: I would be soundly defeated.

But on Wednesday, November 24, 1976, I was the front runner on my maiden voyage to a world of hard knocks, hardball, and heavy responsibilities. Mr. Baker was right. If we had won the election it would have been victorious, but by getting that far and then losing in a run-off in an at-large election, we were laying the groundwork to challenge a system that would eventually cave in to create district elections that allowed full participation from all citizens.

The more immediate result of my first political race was that it clearly placed me in a position of community leadership. Before long I was asked to serve on more committees than I could with any chance of having any reasonable influence. From committee participation came board appointments and the push and pull of those stations of service and decision-making.

When integration took place in the south, it happened at the expense of many black schools. In almost every instance, black schools and facilities were abandoned. This was the case in Talladega, as the former site of the West Side School had been deserted. A group called *Community Life Institute* worked to restore the facility, but without city support their efforts were minimized. After working with the mayor and city council, a West Side board was appointed. I was appointed to the board and eventually elected president.

On July 28, 1980, the building was formally named in honor of B. N. Mabra, a former principal of the school, and was officially dedicated as a community center in the heart of the black community. Programs for a high school equivalent diploma, Senior Meals on Wheels, blood pressure and sickle cell anemia screenings, and education took a high priority. Our work inspired others and the project received a lot of positive press.

The Board hired an energetic, personable, and grand-looking woman by the name of Sandra Cameron to serve as Center Director of the Mabra Center. "San" brought to her position the insight of a native Talladegian, exceptional organizational skills, a "can do" mentality, and a special love for the needy. Often networking with her radiant sister, Patricia Graham, a professional in her own right, San kept her eye on the purpose for which the center was dedicated in spite of terrific struggles that seethed within funding sources.

Additionally impressive were the contributions of a capable man by the name of Jerome Curry, who owned property next to the Mabra Center location. Jerome took special pride in our work and provided a host of resources as we faced unanticipated needs.

"They fired her over some crumbs on the floor."

I couldn't believe my ears or my eyes. I sat in a school board meeting from 5 p.m. to 12:30 a.m. It was more a spectacle than a meeting. The egos of a select few determined the course of the day. The meeting resulted in the loss of employment for a lady who had been a wonderful teacher. Mr. Daniel B. Armstrong to this day remains a member of our church deacon board, and at that time was the only minority member of the Talladega City Board of Education. Mr. Armstrong had asked me to attend the meeting and to speak for a form of reprimand that was less than termination for the teacher whose hearing was being held. It revolved around some students having dropped crumbs on the lunchroom floor.

The assistant principal and teacher had had words. The matter got out of control. I was shocked. This was not a matter of moral turpitude, incompetence, or child abuse. I was never allowed to address the board. They listened to attorney arguments. The assistant involved testified that he felt the teacher should not have been terminated. The board deliberated, went into executive session, and returned with a vote of four to one to fire the teacher. The teacher was black. The assistant was black. The only black on the board voted against termination, citing "the punishment is too severe." His arguments fell on deaf ears. The four whites voted to terminate, and a teacher's skills and commitment to children was thus terminated.

After the meeting, Mr. Armstrong and I talked. I tried to encourage him, but he said to me, "I want you to accept this position. My time is almost up. You will be a strong advocate. I will help you. We can get three votes on the city council to appoint you." I gave him my word that I would accept the position if appointed.

Mount Canaan is a church saturated with insightful and courageous people who are committed to change "the things that we can." The word began to buzz around the church. Contacts were made, letters were written, and meetings were set up. The idea became attractive to community civic leaders beyond our church circles. The appointment seemed to be an "event just waiting to happen." Boy, was I wrong.

The Willie Lynch Principle

Sometimes there are moments when you recognize the prompting of a palpable presence, but do not or cannot properly appreciate it because you have no means to evaluate it. It is amazing how a single act or a small bit of information can promote such profound understanding of complex problems that you wonder how you missed seeing before what you can't avoid seeing after.

He came to see me early one Saturday morning. I'd made a pot of coffee and the aroma and taste of freshly perked *Folgers* made my early rising seem like a small price to pay. A late night phone call and an urgent request for this 6 A.M. Saturday morning meeting seemed a bit mysterious.

He arrived promptly at 6 A.M. "Reverend Patterson, I apologize for getting you up so early, but I need to share some very important information with you," he said as his sad eyes seemed to scan my office.

He looked as if he was searching for something that I had overlooked. "I hope your office is not bugged."

I replied, "You can never know about these things, but I think that it's all right."

"You have a lot of people, black and white, worried in this town. They couldn't buy you, harness you, or trap you. You don't have to answer me. I know about the 500 dollar offer. I also know about the woman they sent to try to seduce you. I know her name. She wanted you to meet her in Birmingham, but you said no. By the way, the silk suit that she offered to you as a gift was paid for by them. You wear a forty-two regular."

I interrupted, "Wait a minute. Who are you? Where are you getting your information?"

"You know I'm right. I wouldn't know about this stuff from reading the newspaper or watching T.V."

I leaned over from my seat uncertain of what and who I was dealing with. He knew about the 500 dollar offer from the man who wanted to reopen to Twenty-Four Horsemen for "cat house" purposes. I was, I guess, really shocked when he referred to the female. I had received several phone calls from this attractive young woman who claimed to have had marital problems. I had counseled her. She had a pear-shaped face and wore her deep raven hair as a full crown at the top. It created a symmetry with her facial features. She favored the classic shag hair style which flattered her pear-shaped face. Her soft-colored ivory skin tone coupled with her Jones of New York wardrobe made her very easy on the eyes.

My sense of suspicion prevailed, however, and alerted me to the danger that this woman represented. I knew enough about counseling to figure out that the incongruity that I sensed as she spoke of painful issues was more theatrical than dysfunctional. The expensive suit she offered me reinforced my apprehensions. I had no idea that she was some kind of bait to be used to destroy me, but I did know that she was driven into my presence by forces that were not in my best interest.

When my mysterious guest spoke to me of this woman, I knew that he had access to knowledge that I had only shared with Doe, as I sought her counsel and her prayers.

I swore never to reveal his identity. He pledged to help me in my quest to change Talladega for the better.

Before leaving, he opened an envelope and said, "I have something for you from Willie Lynch."

"Willie who?" I asked, baffled and still somewhat staggering under the weight of the news that he had already shared.

"Willie Lynch is somebody that you've got to deal with." He went on to explain to me that Willie Lynch lived in 1712. He was not only a slave owner, but he was also a slave maker. In 1712, Willie Lynch wrote a letter to his fellow slave owners addressing the subject of how they could best control their slaves:

> Teach them to distrust each other. Pitch the old black male against the young black male. Turn the dark skin slave against the light skin slave. I assure you that distrust is stronger than trust. You must have your white servants and overseers distrust all blacks, but it is necessary that they trust and depend on us. We must teach them to love, respect, and trust us and nobody but us.

In his closing words Willie Lynch wrote, "I guarantee every one of you, if you follow my advice, this method will control your slaves for at least 300 years."

As I shared with this man who had befriended and educated me on the "Willie Lynch principle," my mind raced back to the phone call of the dying white miner who said, "Maybe you don't know it, but white folks always got some colored folks they use to keep folks like you from doing too much." I remembered Mrs. Gussie's lecture to me on the Bourbons and the tolls they used to keep blacks and poor whites out of seats of power. I remembered the emotion in her voice that ranged from anger to excruciating pain when she said, "It was about power and money then and it's about the same thing now. The Bourbons may have changed their names, but their descendants live on. The Ku Klux Klan are just stupid, poor, white people who have more in common with us than they have with the Bourbons."

Willie Lynch did his job well. The Bourbons caught his spirit and passed it on, but without their knowledge, my mysterious friend, had infiltrated their circle of greed and across the years would warn me of their plans and counsel me on ways to thwart their treachery.

The Saturday Night Conspiracy

According to my friend they met on a secluded country estate. It was a strange mixture. There were three representatives from the old money regime. They never ran for political office, but they often decided who got elected. They were seldom in the newspapers, but they monitored the influence of those who were, and I had caught their attention. These were the kind of people that the white miner had told me about years ago. They were white. They had money. They called a lot of shots. They made a lot of things happen and they kept a lot of things from happening.

There was the black man who wanted to reopen the Twenty-Four Horsemen facility for "cathouse" purposes. He had five people with him, two men and three women. He had grown obsessed with my destruction. Every achievement that I realized was like a dagger pricking his heart. His prophecy had not only remained unfulfilled, but it seemed as if it might not ever escalate into the demise of my leadership. By this time, I had become Talladega College's director of tutorial services. I had also built a new home and Doe had given birth to our second son, Julian Niles (Jay).

Jay P., as we have affectionately called him, came into our lives with dancing eyes and a mischievous grin. Having inherited large locks of curly hair from my father, Jay's oval-shaped face and gentle heart made him our smiling gift from God. Horace Jr. wanted to name him Rodimus Prime, some Star Wars or G.I. Joe character I believe, but Doe and I overruled him.

Horace Jr. had a little brother. Mount Canaan proudly boasted of another member of her first family. Doe and I simply bowed our heads in unspeakable gratitude for that expression of heavenly kindness.

Life for our family had little stress at that time, and the very thought that I was a shoe-in for the school board made my enemy and his cohorts miserable.

This gang of nine came together on that beautiful spring night three Saturdays before the Board of Education appointment was to be made. The catfish was frying. The grounds were manicured. The beer was cold, but the mood was not festive.

The old money representatives set the tone, saying, "Ladies and gentlemen, we have a problem. This Patterson fellow is becoming too influential. I thought that you folks told us that y'all could handle things. Now we hear he's built a house to stay here, raising a ton of money in that church to do some building work, just been on the damn front page of the paper dedicating that old school, and now is about to get appointed to the school board. What y'all been doing? Running some kind of 'Let's Crown Patterson King campaign?'"

One of the women said, "It's not our fault. It was that Willoford thing. He came out of that mess looking like a hero. I still don't know how he did it."

The "Willoford thing" referred to a black man who introduced himself to the black Talladega community as John Willoford. Willoford—I doubt that was his real name—was a crooked con man. He claimed to have grown up in Chapel Hill, North Carolina, and had strong government ties in Washington, D.C. as a pantyhose manufacturer. He claimed to have been in Talladega looking to purchase property for the purpose of building a plant that would initially employ one thousand people. He used the old "something great for a little" con and had secured "partners" from all over the community. It was the "don't tell anybody, but I like you and I am going to let you get in on the ground floor" scheme. He had taken advantage of several members of my parish. They introduced him to me and asked that he be allowed to hold some community meetings in our church.

I reluctantly agreed, but after listening to him I withdrew our church facilities from his use. Willoford knew the law. He was smug and arrogant at times. He was smooth and he was an impressive speaker. He dropped a lot of big names, but it was all fluff with no substance. He used scriptures, phony papers, and a host of promises to take advantage of some very good people. He was out of my league. I contacted the police. Mr. Wilby Wallace, a soloist in our church, was acting police chief. Chief Wallace threatened Willoford, but without witnesses and sworn complaints, no legal action could be taken. Yes, Willoford was out of my league, but I knew just the right somebody.

I called Coronad Johnson, my old Air Force buddy from St. Louis. He gave me some great advice.

Another Air Force buddy, who we fondly called Stockdale, flew in and set up a meeting with two men whom I trusted without reservations. Arthur Jackson, a retired educator and businessman at that time, and Walter Baker, a retired electrician, were both deacons in our church who lent their skills and resources to help con the con man.

Stockdale explained, "The ideal tool to make a con work is always cash. Even though con men know it and use it they are almost always blinded by cold, hard, quick cash."

Arthur Jackson, bright, humorous, and, at times, playful, arranged to get us a private condominium at the plush resort of Alpine Bay—a private resort of elegant condominiums, tennis courts, and swimming pools that were located less than a thirty minute drive from the heart of the city of Talladega. Arthur, in response to the cash hook, said, "I'll tell you now that even though I've got problems, cash ain't one of them. How much do we need?" Walter Baker sat his tall brown frame on a sofa, laughed, and said, "I want all you got."

The con was simple. A meeting with Willoford was set up. Walter Baker pretended, with false deeds, to want to sell one-hundred acres of property, rich with timber that was ready to cut, because he needed some quick cash.

Arthur and another party claimed that Willoford had been highly recommended by people throughout the community, but some honest money had to be put up front. It was marketed as a win-win situation.

When Arthur opened his briefcase, Willoford almost choked at the sight of cold cash. The honest money figure, that Arthur had brought, had to be matched by Willoford. Arthur started at 25,000 dollars each. The final figure that Willoford could produce was only 3,000 dollars in the twenty-four-hour time frame in which the deal was offered. The timber alone, in the scheme marketed to Willoford, was valued at over 200,000 dollars.

The con man got conned. We were only able to give back a few hundred dollars to those from whom Willoford had taken. We returned the little that had been gotten and Willoford, knowing that his cover was blown, took off, never to return. The few people that we were able to help were eternally grateful.

Arthur Jackson and Walter Baker made certain, in their own quiet way, that people knew of my involvement and those persons became loyal supporters of my work.

So when the woman referred to the "Willoford thing," she was also referring to a group of people whose cause I had championed with a little financial success and their immeasurable gratitude.

As the evening wore on, the gang of nine decided to attack me in several areas in order to prevent my school board appointment. They would raise the outsider issue among native-born Talladegians. This attempt would elicit the envy of others by saying that outsiders were coming in and taking over the town. Why should somebody from Bessemer be placed in that seat of power?

This, of course, was the old divide-and-conquer mentality. It had been historically effective. Why not run it up the flagpole and see who would continue to salute it?

Next, they would attack my character. After the meeting was over, the blacks were to immediately start a rumor that I had been caught in a married woman's bed by her husband. The lie had to be both juicy and specific. The lie said that I had been caught, had fought with the husband in his home, and had been arrested and booked in jail at 12 a.m. that Sunday morning. Each component of the lie could and would fall apart. The idea, of course, was not to defend that which would fall beneath the weight of scrutiny, but to just throw something against the walls, with the hope that something would eventually stick in the minds of my supporters in order to create doubt and destroy their enthusiastic support of my school board appointment.

They would also advance the idea that preachers should not be involved in issues that were political. While this weak argument was divorced from the African-American historical reality of ministerial involvement, it was advanced with vigor. The fact that each of the six blacks who were present received 500 dollars to launch these attacks probably had a lot to do with their zeal. For five hundred dollars the six blacks who attended the Saturday night conspiracy went forth with the industry and zeal of missionaries.

The three whites were to call city council members and try to turn their votes, by saying that I would push for a breakfast program for children because a lot of blacks were too lazy to get up and feed their own children. The fact that the breakfast program would serve all children was never discussed. The correlation between proper nutrition and academic achievement was also never mentioned. The reality that hungry children don't learn well was a non-issue to them; they were concerned with politics and anger, not children. This attempt was designed in order to convince the council that they needed to appoint someone who would "work with them" and was advanced repeatedly.

For three long weeks both my supporters and my antagonists butted heads. On the Sunday morning following the Saturday night conspiracy meeting, members of my parish greeted me and informed me of the host of phone calls that had been made regarding the lie about me and a married woman, the outsider issue, and ministerial limitation arguments. Some laughed and told me that their only response to their callers was, "Do you think I'm that stupid?" followed by a prompt hang-up. Some were hurt for me and simply said, "Be strong. You're in my prayers. Don't worry. We know better." Some became angry and said, "This is just the same soup warmed over. When the Lord builds a church, the devil builds a chapel, and when a strong man shows up, the snakes crawl from under their rocks." Some simply said, "It just makes me want to cuss."

The overwhelming majority of the congregation remained steadfast.

A few changed. I could see it on their faces, observe it in their stares, and hear it in their voices. They were only a few, but even as a few they made me aware of the mounting cost that I would have to pay in emotional currency as I moved toward another level of leadership. Those few also served as a constant reminder to me of the unique stock of the majority of those courageous and insightful people that I had been called to serve at Mt. Canaan.

The gang of nine failed. In April of 1981, I received the appointment to the Talladega Board of Education. I would serve for ten years as a member, and three of those years as the first African-American school board president. I had no idea, however, that my appointment to the board would result in a politically embarrassing and vindictive termination.

5

The Board of Education

I WAS WELL received by the majority of the sitting school board members in 1981. There appeared to have been a real desire to resolve issues without controversy. One aging elementary school had become 98 percent black. We all knew that this was not good because it served as a residual postscript to the days of segregation and all of its inherent evils. In Alabama, separate was never equal. Black schools were always under-funded and understaffed. We closed that school and built a two-million-dollar facility to replace it. We had the opportunity to celebrate the retirement of one superintendent and the hiring of another. We worked as a unit.

Eventually, we were able to start breakfast programs and open up administrative positions for able minority administrators. In a school system that was 45 percent African-American, eight administrative positions were filled by only two minorities. When I became a school board member, one position was a building principal. The other was an assistant superintendent. As school board members during the early eighties, we worked to remedy those ills. There were times when the vote was four to one, but we generally sought to avoid issues that polarized the community.

The issue of the use of conduct grades to keep students off the honor roll was an exception to our show of unity. I was fast approaching a state where I wondered if the dropout rate was, in reality, a push-out rate that started in elementary school. I was deeply disturbed because I'd seen several students with all A's in classwork subjects, but unable to make the honor roll because of a C in conduct. A math problem's answer is not subjective, but the rating of a child's conduct is. There were numerous complaints. Some children could do the same thing in the same class before the same teacher and nothing happened, while others reaped punitive consequences. I argued my position and lost. It did not make me very popular with some of the teachers who passionately supported the use of conduct grades in order to determine a child's eligibility for honor roll status. They claimed that it was a necessary tool for discipline. I continued to believe that there are numerous ways to modify behavior without chilling academic enthusiasm.

The teachers favoring conduct grades employed a very interesting and creative approach. All of the teachers who openly favored doing so were white, but on the night of the school board meeting, they had recruited two black female parents to advocate their position. Donald and Keith Mfume, the stalwart sons of Kweisi Mfume, president and C.E.O. of the NAACP, have been quoted as saying, "As African-American men, we were often told by our father that people would always assume that we were ignorant until we spoke. It was only then that we could either prove them right or prove them wrong." Sometimes the opposite assumption of intelligence is also made simply because of appearances.

On the day of the conduct grade confrontation, I erroneously assumed that I had an ally. She was one of the two black women chosen to speak by the teachers. She appeared to be in her mid-thirties. She wore a dark business suit with a light-colored blouse. Her neck was laced with a single strand of pearls. She had the appearance of being professional, insightful, and tactful. When her turn to speak came around, I was shocked.

She repeatedly said, "I support the teachers because I want somebody to teach my children how to act. I don't care about the subjects. I want somebody to teach my children how to act."

I wanted to remind her that that was her job as a parent, but I was taken by surprise. Even though the auditorium was packed to capacity, my eyes found Doe's eyes. She sympathetically looked at me with one of those "I can't believe this" looks and then looked upward. Our frustration stemmed from the fact that the very same young women who had just finished espousing the virtues of the conduct grades approach had been in contact with me on several occasions, seeking counseling for some of the very same problems that came as a result of subjective and partial treatment of children.

Every day in this country children are labeled as dropouts who in fact have been pushed from their early school years out of the schools because of subjective and partial treatment. What makes this matter so troubling is that some parents are more prone to follow the dictates of people rather than work for the evenhanded application of policies that require objective appraisals.

Larry Barton

Larry Barton had worked as a banker. He first secured overwhelming African-American voter support in the city of Talladega for mayor in the summer of 1979, and began his term in October of that same year. He was gregarious, impressive, and extremely popular. Elected mayor for three terms, Larry Barton was viewed as an able administrator and a strong politician. I actively campaigned on his behalf on two occasions and passionately worked to defeat him on another. Time would eventually usher me into a state of direct conflict with him that would make political support or opposition appear mild, as an entire city became caught up in a crisis that would warrant the attention of the *Wall Street Journal*.

1983 was saturated with a great deal of promise for our city. The school board was working in harmony and City Hall was quiet. Vanessa Williams had been crowned Miss America and of all things, she was invited to be the grand marshal of the Talladega City Christmas parade. She accepted the invitation. It was an exciting time for the whole city. The excitement transcended communities.

By 1983, my personal life took a turn for the better. After years of dedicated and rewarding servicer, I moved from Talladega College to accept a position in community mental health. My coworkers, clients, and friends were all mesmerized by the wonderful news. Miss America was coming to Talladega. It was, for most of us, a once-in-a-lifetime experience. In welcoming her to the city, the mayor ceremoniously presented her with the traditional key to the city. It was all good.

In September 1984, when the *Penthouse* 15th anniversary issue featured Vanessa Williams with George Burns on the cover titled "*Oh, God. She's nude!*" A sense of sorrow overwhelmed many of us. The black-and-white nude photographs taken by Tom Chiapel, prior to her role as reigning queen, revealed an erotic and flamboyant young woman. They took back her crown, and Larry Barton sought to take back the key to the city of Talladega.

It was a hot Thursday afternoon. The phone rang and Horace Jr. said, "Dad, it's the mayor."

After our customary greetings he said, "I'm thinking about asking Vanessa Williams to return the key to the city. You know how strongly I feel about pornography." I agreed with his stand on the sale of material that could be labeled as pornographic. He had championed an ordinance that had been passed into law—making the sale of pornographic material illegal within the city limits. I responded by saying, "Mr. Mayor, I applaud your stand on pornography, but I can't see how asking Miss Williams to return a key that doesn't fit anything can advance the crusade against pornography."

"Have you seen those nude pictures that she took?"

"No."

"I have. They are sick. I bought a magazine and took it to my church to let the people see for themselves. Do you want to see them?"

"No, I don't want to see them," I said. "If they are as bad as you say, I don't see why you want to show them and I really don't understand why you would take them into a church. People make mistakes. She has already suffered enough. They've taken her crown. I think that we all will be better served to pray for her and her family and leave the matter of the key alone. Besides, it doesn't fit anything and it's like stepping on someone when that person is down."

"I don't agree. I'm going to get that key."

"Mr. Mayor," I replied, "I hope that you will leave this unhappy event alone. If you persist in it I will not support you, and nor will I support you when you run for office again. You've just been reelected. Be thankful. Black folks have been good to you. Don't take us for granted or use us for political grandstanding."

"I don't understand you. All the other blacks support me on this."

"I can't speak for others," I said, "but I will tell you that this thing is wrong and wrong is just wrong. It's looking like, quacking like, walking like, and smelling like a duck, and if it looks, quacks, walks, and smells like a duck, then it probably is a duck."

"If that's how you feel, good-bye."

I really hoped that he wouldn't persist. Vanessa Williams had been through enough, and even if he played this issue for political gain, I was determined that he would not do it with my blessings. Ms. Williams's actions, and mistakes, were her own as far as I was concerned.

The mayor wrote a letter asking Vanessa Williams to return the key to the city, and it became a media event. I am not certain of the specifics of how a personal letter became a media circus, but it did. The national media picked up on it and soon it became an international disaster for the image of our city. The BBC wanted an interview, and the story about a Talladega, Alabama, mayor who asked Miss America to return the key to the city was carried by the *London Times*. While the mayor said that the matter was a part of his moral crusade against pornography, I found it suspicious that during this same time period, he announced his candidacy for the statewide lieutenant governors' race on the Republican ticket.

My approach to living is summed up by the belief system which says, "We are called to worship God, love people, and use things." When we start to worship ourselves, we will use people and love things. Taking the issue out of the volatile realm of partisan politics, I felt that Vanessa had paid her penance. She had suffered enough. She had been hurt and it pained me that the city of Talladega was somehow being connected with pouring the proverbial salt into the wound. I spoke about it and I preached against it. A few people in the community resented my position. A few people in our church told me to "be careful." I received several phone calls from some misguided but well-meaning people who urged me to "lighten up."

I didn't. Soon our city became a national joke over a key that didn't fit anything. The mayor did not win his bid for lieutenant governor, and I actually lost some support from some black people and gained some support from the white community. While I have never believed in letting polls dictate matters of conscience, I was, nevertheless, curious about the dynamics. The stage had been set for a political confrontation for the next mayoral race. Some expected me to run for mayor. I had no desire to do so. My school board work was fulfilling and our church was doing great. Before long, we would complete a quarter-of-a-million-dollar education facility. We were working in phases and things couldn't be better.

Doe, What Is a "Crazy Check?"

It was a rainy Tuesday night. As the evening deepened, the rain drops slashed against the windows with alternating velocity. The meeting had been long and at times boring. Not many people care to attend a school board meeting that focuses on the upcoming fiscal budget. Finally, after answering a lot of questions that nobody was asking, we adopted the budget.

A black man in a rear seat against the wall sat through the nerve-wracking process unaffected as we spoke of capital outlay expenditures and state mandated employee raises. He was attired in a white short sleeve shirt and dark trousers. He only glanced at us intermittently, as he seemed to finger through a booklet of papers. His face spoke of determination.

I could tell, as his eyes met mine, that this man not only wanted something from me, but he was willing to wait to receive it.

At the close of the meeting, he made his way toward me and introduced himself as a retired army sergeant. He and his wife had received custody of their three grandchildren. Their daughter, the mother of the children, was in drug rehabilitation. I could hear the disappointment in his voice as he spoke. The children's father was in federal prison for drug trafficking.

The story grew sadder as he told it. All three children had been tested and labeled mentally retarded. The sergeant said as he held his hand against his cheek, "I think we are getting some crazy checks."

"Crazy checks?" I said.

"Yeah, that's why I've come to see you. A few months before I retired, I read a story in a magazine about crazy checks. The article said some parents had pushed for their children to be labeled mentally retarded because they qualified for money from the government. We've just taken the kids and one gets a check for almost a 1,000 dollars a month and the other two get almost 500 dollars apiece, each month. I don't think that these kids are mentally retarded. I don't know where to start or what to do. I need your guidance. I don't know what this means to their future, but as an old soldier, I know there ain't no free lunches. Sooner or later somebody always has to pay. I don't want these kids to have to pay for their parents' greed like some children I've seen."

"What do you mean?" I asked.

"When I was in Korea many years ago I saw parents who begged for a living. They would cut, deface, and even break the bones of their own children in order to get more money because people would be more sympathetic in their giving. I just don't want my grandchildren's future sacrificed for a few dollars."

"I understand," I said. "I'll do some research and get back to you."

It was a troubling condition. I went home. I knew that Doe could help. She served as a member of the Multi-disciplinary Eligibility Committee for our school system. This committee determined admissions criteria and placement for special education services. After greeting her and the kids, Doe and I sat down. I asked her to tell me about crazy checks.

She smiled. "What do you want to know? Are you interested in applying for one? Because if you do, I am convinced that there are some days that you might qualify without difficulty."

We laughed and I agreed. After a few light moments of joking, I returned to my question, and what she said moved me to do additional research and raise some serious questions.

The law states that a child will be considered disabled if he or she has a physical or mental condition, or a combination of conditions, that results in "marked and severe functional limitations." Through Supplemental Security Income supplements, children can qualify for monthly income if they meet the Social Security definition of disability. To determine a child's eligibility, a check is made to see if the child's disability can be found in a special listing of impairments that is contained in Social Security regulations. There are more than 100 physical and mental problems that are listed as being severe enough to disable a child. In most public school settings, those areas that warrant admission for these special services are specific learning disabilities, mental retardation, emotional conflict, traumatic brain injury, and speech impairment.

A student labeled with any of these disabilities qualifies for payments. A student could be labeled mentally retarded and emotionally conflicted. This would provide a second monthly payment because additional income is provided for each exceptionality. My research soon revealed a disturbing pattern.

Most minorities receiving special services were labeled mentally retarded. Most white students receiving special services were labeled as learning disabled. Students who are labeled mentally retarded are placed in self-contained classrooms, and receive a subsequent stigma from peers. They do not generally receive a diploma, but a certificate of completion.

Learning disabled students are not placed in a self-contained classroom. They remain in the mainstream of school life and activities. These students receive accommodations without receiving the stigma attached to mentally retarded students. Learning disabled students who graduate generally receive a high school diploma.

The terminology of crazy checks came about because many students appeared to have been coached to fail certain tests in order to qualify for

SSI benefits. I called my brother-in-law, Marion McIntosh, an educator in a south Alabama school system, and asked for his insights on the matter. Marion said that there are students who play crazy to get a check. "I can recall one who laughingly told me," he said, "'I get paid for acting a fool. Every chance I get I put the head of a donkey at his tail and the tail of a donkey at his head. Call me crazy, but man, I get paid.'"

I reported my findings to the sergeant. I also discovered that children could be dismissed from special education service upon parental request and student improvement. The sergeant and his family relocated to another state and at my last contact, all three children were doing well in regular classrooms. From that time, I have taken every advantage of every opportunity to educate parents about the pitfalls and downsides that could accompany any crazy checks. The sergeant was right: "There ain't no free lunches."

Children who deserve these services and benefits ought to have them. Children who are coached by greedy parents and/or guardians are being taken advantage of. I have spoken, lectured, preached, and counseled with the goal of remedying that disconcerting setup. It made some people very uncomfortable. I knew that it did, but my future would not be worth very much if I remained silent over an issue that has such serious consequences for children.

I remembered an incident in the life of Dr. King that called for "courageous abandon." People were trying to keep him away from a certain city. They informed him of the threats that had been hurled against his life. He replied, "The issue is not what will happen to me if I go, the real issue is what will happen to those needy people if I don't go." With a lump in my throat, I plowed ahead. I sought to impact upon the systematic misapplication of admissions in special programs, while at the same time raising the consciousness level of parents regarding what such a ploy meant to their children's future.

Grade Retention

Whoever said, "So much to do and so little time to do it" must have served on a school board, I told myself. In a small town, a chance meeting at the grocery store can turn into the answer to somebody's prayer. Such was the case for the lady who stopped me one autumn evening in Winn Dixie. I seldom tell Doe that I'm going to the store and will be back in a few minutes, but that's what happened on the day this lady stopped me. She was the mother of two children. One had been retained in the first grade and she informed me that the teacher wanted to retain her second child in kindergarten. As she talked, I wondered, "How can you fail building blocks?"

I listened to her anguish and found her to be well read and most insightful. After an hour somewhere between the fruit and vegetable display, we anchored, determined not to give parental permission for her child to be retained in kindergarten, and I referred her to my education specialist in our church for tutorial assistance. Something didn't seem right about this issue.

Once again, I deferred to Doe. The issue of grade retention was one that she approached with a great deal of passion. As a school board member, I had raised questions concerning our district's response in remedying academic deficiencies. The national thrust at that time, as it is now, was "no more social promotion." Among the panaceas suggested for achieving school improvement is a strict promotion-by-merit policy. A search of the educational research literature has not supported the view implied in that recommendation, that the retention of pupils in grades will lead to more achievement. Students have been and are still being retained despite the research findings.

Doe felt so strongly about the matter that she completed a dissertation for her doctorate degree from the University of Alabama addressing "The Impact of Grade Retention on K-5 Elementary Students."

Researchers have consistently found a significant relationship between grade retention and dropping out. Dropouts are five times more likely to have repeated a grade than are high school graduates. Students who repeat two grades have a probability of dropping out of nearly 100 percent. One study revealed that students who repeated a year were 20 to 30 percent more likely to drop out of school, but African-American males with identical achievement scores who repeated a year in school had a 75 percent chance of leaving school before graduation.

Retention not only has a negative effect on student achievement, but on the emotional aspect of students as well. We discovered a study done by a brilliant researcher by the name of Yamamoto (1980) which revealed that children rated going blind or losing a parent as the two life-threatening events that would be more stressful than being retained.

I was amazed at those revelations and the fact that they had gone unnoticed by so many people who labeled themselves as educators. As I surveyed the emotional currency paid by students who were retained, their self-esteem seemed to drop and die right before my eyes.

Retaining a student is far more costly than the alternatives, which consist of before and after-school tutorial programs, summer school attendance, additional classroom aides to provide one-on-one assistance, and special weekend tutorial assistance.

Retention doesn't work. It destroys children's self-esteem. It is more costly than alternatives, yet it still continues to take place. It is said that the seven last words of a dying church are: "We never did it this way before." I guess you can say the same thing about some school districts. Especially when you have teachers that want to retain children in kindergarten. What we consistently label as the dropout rate may very well be a push-out rate, with the national practice of retention doing a whole lot of the pushing. Dropping out is something a student does to him or herself. Being pushed out is something that is done to the student, and it has to stop.

As a Thursday autumn morning passed, the face of retention crystallized before me while I walked the hall corridors of one of our elementary schools.

He was seated in a desk chair in the hallway because he had been labeled as disruptive in the classroom. His name was Bobby. He was a thinly built white child with sad eyes that spoke of rejection, disappointment, and even horror, his hair unbrushed, his clothing clean but torn and well worn.

He tipped the front legs of his desk toward the classroom door. He seemed to strain as he kept his eyes peeled to see and decipher the message whispered to him from the two voices within the classroom.

"You are nothing but po' white trailer-park-trash," one voice said.

"Yeah, you've been left behind two grades. You're just trailer-park trash," replied the second whispered voice from within.

"Go to hell!" Bobby said as his words rushed through his clenched teeth and his eyes turned liquid with tears.

Bobby sat back in his desk chair with his shoulders dropped as if he was resigned to sit in the debris of his shattered self-esteem.

Unnoticed, I cleared my throat to alert him of my presence and then I approached him. "Is something wrong?" I asked as compassionately as I could.

"No sir," he replied as he quickly rubbed from his eyes the fluid vestiges of his painful encounter.

"What's going on? Why are you in the hallway?" I asked. He said nothing, but dropped his head as a prize fighter who no longer had the will to defend himself might.

I entered the classroom. The teacher, absorbed in her class assignments, was unaware of the dialogue that had taken place between Bobby and the two voices that had labeled him trailer-park-trash. I discovered that the whispering had come from two attractively dressed white girls.

As I surveyed the scene, I took notice of the fact that the label trailer-park trash crushed Bobby's self-esteem in the same way in which a tidal wave crushes the fragile sand castles that a child might build on a beach.

I knew Bobby's hurt. It had happened to me in a different decade. For Bobby it was trailer-park trash. For me it was the voice that cried, "Mama, Mama, look at the niggers." There is a common scar left on the soul that seeks itself out in others. The scar can seal a bond of kinship or it can repel us to look away as one might turn aside from bloated roadkill.

From that day on, I was never free from the face of Bobby as I sought to help many children who were forced to wear labels that they didn't deserve.

A Season of Change

In May of 1987, Doe gave birth to Ivy. The birth of sons is like the shout that comes from a trumpet. The birth of a daughter is like the softness that flows from a flute. Spending my lunch breaks looking for G.I. Joe characters for Horace and Jay was often therapeutic and very special. It was a "Daddy thing" and the looks on their faces when I arrived with new ones were always reward enough.

There are some degrees of appreciation that I gained for my father only after God gave me sons of my own. As my sons rejoiced in their gifts from me, I recalled a treasure from my father that I had not given a great deal of thought to.

Every afternoon when Daddy returned from working in the mines, I would run to the car and take his lunch box. He would always have something in it for me—a piece of an apple, a half of a sandwich, a piece of cake, pie, or candy bar. The treats that came from Daddy's lunch box were better than anything we had in the house or could have been bought at the store. When I ate my treat, I just took it for granted that my daddy always had more than he could eat for lunch. It never dawned on me that, regardless of how hungry he might have been, he always saved something, on purpose, just for me.

As I thought of this unselfish act, tears welled up in my eyes, and I hoped and prayed that I could be as much of a father to my children as Daddy had been to me, even though we had to say goodbye too soon.

The arrival of Ivy awakened an even deeper capacity for tenderness in my heart. The look. The smile. The hugs. The fragility of a daughter, I think, inspires greater strength in a father.

Doe and I worked hard to make sure that our children enjoyed being kids. But even as we enjoyed barbecuing and condominium retreats to Gulf Shores, we wanted and wished that all kids could enjoy being kids. Those wishes continued to inspire my private moments and drive my public decisions.

In the spring of 1987, Dr. Charles A. Tunstall, chairman of the Trustee Board, and Dr. B. W. Dawson, president of my beloved Selma University, recruited me as a candidate for the doctoral degree from Selma University. In partial fulfillment for the conferring of the degree, I was asked to complete two tasks—establish a school of theology extension center in our area for the training of ministers and other church leaders, and write a book introducing a Christian theory to counseling. It was a rich menu. I was excited and honored. Both tasks were important and each in its own way afforded me unique opportunities to serve others.

In the summer of 1987, the city elections took place. True to my word, I did not support the incumbent. He was popular among the African-American church community. Having been an accomplished pianist and recording artist, the mayor had strong political support. I, personally, felt that the Vanessa Williams incident was a community embarrassment. It had been unnecessary and it did not generate the image I felt was in our city's best interest. Apparently most of the Talladegans who voted in the city election of 1987 had similar feelings.

I publicly endorsed George Montgomery, a long-time city clerk. My phone rang off the hook. There were some serious threats made, but by that time I was used to them.

Four weeks prior to the election, I arose one morning and prepared to go to church only to find two of my car tires slashed. During that same week, we discovered our two-month-old German Shepherd puppy, Skippy, had been poisoned to death.

I had given Skippy to Horace Jr. and Jay as a gift. Beaming with life, love, and full of energy, Skippy had quickly won all of our hearts. As I looked at his motionless frame, I recoiled at the sick thoughts fermented in the mean-spirited mind that was at work. Two boxes of rat poison were left in Skippy's pen along with a can of Alpo that we never purchased.

It seemed clear that the forces that were at work wanted me to appraise the full breadth of their treachery. It was the language of evil spoken in a dialect that was not difficult to decode.

After filing a police report and having taken Skippy to the vet to determine the cause of death, Horace Jr. spoke. He looked at me with wide, angry, and baffled eyes and asked, "Dad, how could somebody be that mean? Skippy wasn't bothering anybody. How could somebody poison a puppy?"

"Sometimes people can be cruel," was my response to him while I wrestled with similar questions of my own.

As the election neared, I discovered the fact that there are times when shepherds bleed. But even as the threats increased, I was buoyed by glorious worship services within the walls of our church. Solos from Wilby Wallace's powerful soul-stirring tenor voice, duets from deaconess Imogenge Armstrong and Flora Rhoden singing, "Only What You Do For Christ Will Last" and the matchless renditions of "Some Day I Shall Be Free" sung from the soprano voice and anointed soul of Rosa Strickland lifted me and made our congregational unity seem invincible.

Not unnerved, but angered by another incident, I worked like a Trojan to elect George Montgomery. Around 10:30 one morning after my public endorsement, Jay was playing in the driveway, and a truck smashed a brick fixture in our yard. The bricks flew everywhere. Only a few chips hit Jay and he was fine, but Doe called my office and I rushed home. While the matter was labeled an accident, Doe and I both found it to be a curious accident, especially in light of the previous threats.

Led by Robert Morris, a deacon in our church and a protective friend of my family, several of the men in our church and community responded by patrolling and pulling guard duty at our home.

It was a nasty election. George Montgomery won. We all hoped that this election would mark the beginning of a more progressive climate for our city. There were a few people whose resentment towards me escalated into hatred. The aftermath of my endorsement created a sometimes dangerous world for me. There was much more involved in that election than votes. It was a matter of control. Some thought (and perhaps still think) that the black community could be controlled by going to churches and making speeches—empty words without any real respect. I had been taught that real respect is behavioral, not just verbal. It was also a matter of the black community choosing its own leadership rather than having that leadership chosen by those who did not live among us.

I pulled into a Chevron service station for gas. There might have been thirty minutes worth of daylight remaining and it was paling. They pulled in behind me—two, middle age white males. They drove an old crimson Chevy truck loaded with Confederate regalia. A sign on the drivers' side portrayed a picture of a confederate flag with the words "Keep it Flying" on it. The one who remained by the truck had no facial hair. He was a man of average height who seemed to be along for the ride and he eyed me anxiously from a distance of two car lengths.

The other man was portly built featuring a scraggly beard. He walked over towards me. He was wearing a gray T-shirt decked with the picture of an old confederate soldier standing above the words "Forget Hell." The moment, present with hostility, seemed to rise in tension as he stretched his fat little right hand open and close while hitting it against the open palm of his left hand.

"You're Patterson, ain't you?"

"I looked at him and said, "That's my name."

"You messed us up in that election," he said. "We know what to do with your kind."

I remained standing behind my car door and looked him directly in the eyes and asked, "Tell me. What do you do with my kind?"

Before he could answer, Johnny Clark, a black National Guard staff sergeant whose features portray a military bearing, and Johnny Harris, a deacon in our church with the heart of a lion, arrived on the scene simultaneously and greeted me with warm hellos. Whether their arrival was planned or by chance I cannot say, but it was clear that their arrival unnerved the unwelcome stranger who had confronted me.

Sensing that I was not afraid and not alone, he whispered some vulgarity, walked off, and sped away. It was a silly attempt to intimidate me. I knew from my civil right days that you don't fear talkers who talk in the daylight when witnesses are everywhere. The Bible said it best: "Those who do evil love darkness."

In the spring of 1988, I had a visit at my church from the Talladega County commission chairman, Frank Strickland, and the chairwoman of the Retired Senior Volunteer Program, Mrs. Mildred Maxwell. They informed me that the physical condition of the present director of the program was rapidly failing. I provided some consultation work for them at no cost.

Mr. Strickland said, "There are some people really after you. I know you can take care of yourself, but we'd really like to have your skills heading up this program."

At that time I had graduated from Jacksonville University, in Jacksonville, Alabama, with a master of science degree in counseling. After having spent several rewarding years as a psychotherapist and supervisor in the clinical mental health arena, I had been named director of the chronic care division.

The charge given to the chronic care division was to provide community care (medication management, group, family, and/or individual therapy) for persons who had experienced a history of mental illness that warranted institutionalization. The driving mission to keep those clients stable enough to remain in the community proved to be both emotionally worthy and fiscally responsible.

I had designed, with great success, a geriatric program and had been invited to speak about it at several civic club luncheons. Both Mrs. Maxwell, a retired educator, and Mr. Strickland, who had been part owner of a mortuary that bore his name, had been present at a luncheon held in Anniston, Alabama, where I had spoken.

I sincerely thanked both of them for their kind support and commitment to the seniors of Talladega County.

Mr. Strickland, sitting in one of my burgundy office chairs horizontal to my desk, cupped his face as he buried it in his hands. He seemed so struck with conflicting emotions that he barely spoke as he struggled to sort them out.

"Think over our offer. It will be good for you and we really need your skills. Jack worked too hard for us to let this program dissolve," he said as he seemed to fight off the words I sensed he really wanted to say. He was referring to Jack Seals. Jack spoke with a strong drawl and had been a strong advocate for senior services for more than twenty years. Standing over six feet tall with blue eyes and thin brown hair, Jack's declining health eventually overruled his passion to head up the program that he loved so dearly.

In the fall of 1988, I left my post as director for mental health. By that time, the gang of nine had grown to a crowd of twenty-seven, according to inside information given to me by my secret friend who had infiltrated the "Patterson haters." I was concerned for his safety. The people that I had been disturbing were dangerous. He listened to my advice but continued to keep me informed. He now lives with God. I miss him and I owe him. There are days when I sense him still looking over me from his seat in Heaven.

The now-gang of twenty-seven were meeting regularly. They had spent a lot of money trying to destroy me and had failed. As director of mental health for chronic care, I had philosophical differences and administrative conflicts. After I left, the crowd of twenty-seven, composed of the old money representatives, the cathouse cohorts, political enemies, and their recruits spent 10,000 dollars in one month to spread lies. They started the wildest rumors that they could think of. They said that I had been fired from Chronic Care because I had embezzled 20,000 dollars and that I would be arrested within sixty days. They said that I had gotten a seventeen-year-old white girl pregnant, that I had been caught having sex with little boys, and that I had become addicted to crack cocaine.

The rumors were rampant. The payees earned their pay. Their job was to tell it to every source that would listen. I was in a war that had no rules. It was not only difficult, it was painful. I watched as people I had helped took the blood money and spread the filth.

One Monday afternoon as I walked across the Wal-Mart parking lot, I sensed eyes upon me. I turned and there she was, staring scornfully. She was an ebony-skinned woman with an oval-shaped face in her mid-fifties. I had saved her job with our school system. She had made some very inappropriate remarks to some of her students regarding their parent's behavior when they were her students. She could have been fired. Two administrators and three school board members had joined forces to have her terminated. It was a battle that lasted for two months. On some days, in spite of my best efforts, I felt like I was banging on a jammed door that was unwilling to budge.

Finally, I was able to get enough votes to reprimand her, rather than ending her career. I thought that she would have been a friend for life. I was wrong. As I approached her, I spoke as pleasantly as I could. "Hello," I said.

She bowed her head with disdain in her eyes, but made no sound. She coldly turned away and walked off, as if I had the plague.

I had also befriended a man who needed a chance. He was a hard working, brown-skinned, middle-aged man who had been involved in the purchase of some stolen items. I had gotten him a lawyer who took his case pro-bono. The charges were dropped and he was given a second chance.

He had, according to my secret friend who had infiltrated the circle of my enemies, taken 700 dollars to spread any vicious rumors that he could imagine to destroy me.

One summer night as I completed my three-mile walk at the Spring Street recreation center, I saw him before he recognized me. I spoke and matter-of-factly greeted him with the information that I had received. I chose my words carefully, even as I fought with myself to contain my disappointment and anger.

Shamefaced, he looked at me with a tortured face and said wearily, "People are just lying on me. I got a call from that white lawyer that you got for me and he told me he had heard that I was a Judas. I told him that I wasn't. I was going to call you myself. I was." His body tensed with frustration as his sad eyes seemed glued to the floor. He stood frozen as if his strength had been sapped by my confrontation or his guilt proved too heavy a load to carry.

I ended our interaction and walked off with the deepened conviction that he was lying.

I knew that time would crush the movement, and it was at that time that I began to understand that there are some things you are not meant to prosper from, but to simply survive. Mark Twain once said, "I've never met anyone with a good enough memory to be a successful liar." He was right. The stories eventually became known for what they were. It was devastating and shocking to the crowd of twenty-seven. Before long, I had completed my book and had it nationally published, established a school of theology (which flourishes as the Rushing Springs School of Theology in Sylacauga, Alabama), received my doctoral degree from Selma University, and reshaped the Retired Senior Volunteer Program. As a church, we had burned the mortgage on the quarter-of-a-million-dollar educational building and had begun plans to build apartments.

Eventually, a separate agency had one of the leading law firms in the state of Alabama conduct an investigation into those charges of misconduct. The results were: *"It was verified there were no implications of accusations of Mr. Patterson for any wrongdoing by him. To the contrary, his prior employer spoke highly of Mr. Patterson, of his integrity, judgment, and competence during his tenure."*

The investigation, and the truth that it revealed, sickened my enemies and validated for my friends the fact that I had not betrayed their trust.

We cannot isolate ourselves from the evil about us, but we can insulate our hearts against the evil that is around us. To insulate my heart, I used the words from an unknown writer quoted in Dr. H. Beecher Hicks, Jr.'s book, *"Preaching through a Storm:"*

> Three men are my friends
> He who hates me, He who loves me,
> and He who is indifferent to me.
> He who hates me teaches me caution;
> He who loves me teaches me tenderness;
> He who is indifferent to me teaches me self-reliance.
> Three men are my friends!

By learning caution, tenderness, and self-reliance, I continue to find myself indebted to all the categories of people who have and who continue to affect my life; they have given me determination, focus, goal orientation, and tenacity. I remember when, on June 21, 1986, Don Sutton became the thirtieth major league pitcher to win 300 games. He never pitched a no-hitter and he was traded four times. He wasn't a consistent league leader in strikeouts, but he didn't have to be. He just kept winning baseball games. Don Sutton's success was a modern illustration to me. It was a reminder of the power that comes from purpose. In a small southern town of only 19,000, I see in my struggles a message for the masses and a beacon for agents of change everywhere.

Mrs. Bessie Beck Urquhart, a fair-skinned woman, returned to her beloved Talladega after her retirement as a supervising public health official in New York City. With her return, our church took off in new directions. Mrs. Urquhart reunited with Mount Canaan, the church of her childhood years, and began to use her grant-writing skills. With her guidance we developed a non-profit 501C corporation titled "Lifeline."

Our work met resistance. We applied for grants, loans, and public assistance in our early days only to be turned away ever so politely. We refused to give up and eventually secured $1,378,000 to build eighteen apartments (affordable housing).

We designated the new units as Canaan Estates II. These eighteen new units composed of two- and three-bedroom accommodations are scheduled to be housed on the same five acres of property that served to house our first set of apartments. The victory of our perseverance is a clear example of the fact that "you can eat an elephant if you take a few bites at a time."

J. T. Smith once wrote in the *Buffalo Recess*, "Civil Rights without economic strength is a borrowed event. It can be taken away at any time." He was right. W.E.B. Dubois wrote, "Wherever you spend your money is where you create a job. If you live in Harlem and spend your money in Chicago, you create jobs for people in Chicago. If you are Black and the businesses are run by people who are not black, then these people come in at 9 A.M., leave at 5 P.M., and take the wealth to the communities in which they live."

Government statistics reveal that African-Americans have approximately 280 billion annually of disposable income. This is more money than the annual budget of Canada. African Americans constitute over 12 percent of the national population but own or run fewer than 2 percent of all businesses. There are national figures that indicate that there are

108 business starts for every 1,000 Arabs in America. For Asians, there are 96 starts per 1,000, and there are 64 starts for whites. By contrast, there are only nine starts for every 1,000 African Americans. My hope for Canaan Estates II is that we will not simply develop a financial base that will roughly be valued at close to two million dollars, but that our example will inspire other churches and black organizations to exceed what we've done.

If we, in the small city of Talladega, Alabama, can demonstrate the will to move in this area, with less than 400 active church members, surely those with greater resources can do no less. You don't have to complain about being "last hired and first fired" when you are doing the hiring and the firing. You don't have to march in the streets when you have the financial strength to march into court with the best legal assistance that money can buy when your civil rights are violated. You don't have to complain about black youth unemployment being high when you have the resources to create jobs that prepare young people for life. You don't have to beg for Pell grants and student loans when you have the financial capacity to pick a child from the worst straits of poverty and say to him or her, "study hard, keep your nose clean, be a good citizen, and make a commitment to make the world better and we will fund your college education."

I was only seventeen years old when I first met Dr. Ralph David Abernathy. At that time he was vice president of SCLC and Dr. Martin Luther King's trusted second in command. We had a civil rights meeting at the Sixteenth Street Baptist Church in Birmingham. Dr. Abernathy pointed me out. Why? I never knew.

He asked me to help take up the offering by fetching some trash baskets. The regular offering trays were overflowing with money so I obeyed. When the money was taken to the finance room of the church he directed me to follow. I soon discovered a man packing his pockets with the money that had just been given. I confronted him. The elderly man, tired and embarrassed, confessed that his family was homeless and hadn't eaten in two days.

I reported the matter to Dr. Abernathy. He said, "Let him have what he needs. The right to swim means nothing to a fish that has no water to swim in." Dr. Abernathy, seemed at that moment in time, to be a prophet whose heart had caught a vision not simply of the stuff that mattered but of the thing that mattered most.

I have seen poor people of all colors, shapes, and sizes but I have only seen black people poor simply because of their race. I have seen justice denied to many people for many reasons but I have only seen black people denied a right that others take for granted—simply because of their race.

To be black and poor is to invite a persecution that never shows mercy. To be black and poor results in exploitation, rejection, and the getting of a lot of jobs that will never allow one to work his or her way out of poverty.

The creation of wealth that is reinvested in the black community is the only vehicle that will enable a people's ongoing journey to restore that which was lost. The amazing lesson that I have learned is that this work is a work that both blacks and whites ought to be engaged in, in order to save our nation. Long ago the National Basketball Association figured out that the best way to save and make the NBA prosper was to strengthen the teams with the poorest winning record. When the season is over the team with the worst record gets the first chance to pick the best new player. When the worst team is made better, the entire league becomes more competitive. The more competitive the league becomes the more prone people are to watch the games because on any given day any team is capable of defeating any other team. No chain is stronger than its weakest link. When we make the black community strong economically, we make America stronger in every way.

I confess that a fire burns in my soul to see this nation of ours as strong as it can be. I hope that I will live long enough to see hopelessness defeated by hopeful people. Maybe I will, maybe I won't but I find comfort in knowing that what we are doing in Canaan Estates will one day play it's role in the bringing about of what Dr. King called "The beloved community."

TALLADEGA AND TALLADEGA COLLEGE

ABOVE: The historic Talladega square and courthouse. Today, major antique stores beckon tourists from around the world. The Talladega International Raceway is a few miles away.
LEFT: the old railroad depot.
BELOW: Talladega College's Savery Library houses the Amistad murals, depicting the successful quest for freedom by captured Africans aboard the slave ship, *The Amistad*.

ABOVE, the Talladega College classes of 1890 and 1891. The college was founded in 1867 by former slaves William Savery and Thomas Tarant and today enjoys a national reputation for academic excellence. It is one of eight four-year historically black colleges and universities in Alabama. BELOW, the school's choir for the years 1893–1894.

Historic Mt. Canaan Baptist Church, founded in 1870, has been deemed a significant landmark by the Alabama Historical Commission and was added to the Alabama Register of Landmarks and Heritage.

Family and Friends

With Coronad Johnson in the United States Air Force, December, 1967, Goose Bay, Labrador.

Doe McIntosh and I were married in June 1970.

Among my best friends are the Rev. Bobby Harris, left, shown as he looked in 1971 as a civil rights activist. He later became the first African American principal of Thompson High School in Shelby County, Alabama, and a two-term city councilman in Alabaster. Bobby has served as pastor of the New Hope Baptist Church in Sylacauga, for more than twenty years.

BELOW, with Willie Muse and Henry Haskins, also in 1971. Dr. Willie Muse ultimately served as president of Selma University and is now president of the Montgomery Bible Institute and Theological center. Rev. Haskins is the Senior Pastor of the Peace and Goodwill Baptist Church in Alexander City. Henry is also a noted national evangelist.

Below, with Doe in 1993.

Clockwise from left: Horace Jr., Jay, and Ivy, 1989; the wedding of Horace Jr. and Angela, December, 2000; our Talladega home, blanketed with a rare snowfall; and with Horace Jr. and Jay while vacationing in Florida, about 1983.

My family, Christmas, 1998.

Talladega Politics and Protests

ABOVE LEFT, Dr. T.Y. Lawrence, the man who should have been superintendent, 1991. Above right, protest leader Eddie Tucker, later twice elected to the Talladega City Council, and president of the Talladega County Democratic Conference. BELOW, Dr. Lawrence at the mass meeting at Mt. Canaan Baptist Church, December 1990.

ABOVE, I have my back to the camera and am sitting next to Dr. T. Y. Lawrence at the standing-room-only school board meeting in January 1991. BELOW, hundreds participated in the protest march to the Talladega City Hall, January, 1991.

A time of confrontation. Pictured in the background: Lillian Lawrence — wife of Dr. T. Y. Lawrence, January 1991. Mrs. Lawrence, a retired educator, had served the Talladega City Board of Education for more than 25 years.

The protests continue. Talladega college students and senior citizens stood together singing "We Shall Overcome." The air was thick with tension but hope was kept alive!

Blacks and whites together, during the T.Y. Lawrence protests, January, 1991.

Demonstration during the T.Y. Lawrence protests. Protest leaders Eddie Tucker and Councilwoman Edythe Seims carrying the picket signs.

With Jesse Jackson at Mt. Canaan Baptist Church, 1992. In the heat of the T.Y. Lawrence protest, I presented Jesse Jackson, as "the man who ought to be president," to a standing-room-only crowd of more than fifteen hundred people.

6

The Man Who Should Have Been School Superintendent

Dr. Thomas Y. Lawrence served the Talladega, Alabama, school system for thirty-one years. He began his career in the city school system as a band director when the city schools were segregated. He worked with children and inspired parents to bake cakes, sell candy, and organize a host of fund-raisers in order to create and maintain an attractive band appearance and travel opportunities for students to visit other Alabama cities. He believed the old Spanish proverb that "poverty does not destroy virtue, nor does wealth bestow it." Dr. Lawrence simply demonstrated moral excellence as he worked and lived. He was a loyal husband and a loving father. He was soft-spoken, polished, insightful, compassionate, hard-working, generous and conscientious. This man was a bridge-builder. He was a remarkable model citizen and able administrator.

A man of average build with a receding hairline and a round face, Dr. Lawrence always seemed to bring a calming presence to the most tempestuous settings.

Dr. Lawrence worked his way from bandleader to teacher. He earned his formal administrative and academic credentials and served as assistant principal, principal, assistant superintendent, and acting superintendent of the city schools on three different occasions. When the city board of education needed him, he was there. He humbly accepted the charges given him and honorably and admirably shouldered them. In times of struggle, he always seemed to have found a clearer sense of who he was and what he wanted to be. I think that it was out of that knowledge of himself that he helped others find the way to their own special arenas of service.

Talladega, Alabama, is located about 105 miles from Montgomery, Alabama, which was the setting of the historical Montgomery bus boycott. Though their experiences were separated by thirty-six years, T. Y. Lawrence and Rosa Parks lived through a common crisis that had brought the two cities much closer than geography and time indicate. Rosa Parks was a hard-working, Christian-hearted woman who had paid for her seat on a bus. She was asked to get up and get out of her seat for one reason—she was black. For thirty-one years, T. Y. Lawrence had paid his dues. He, by merit, had been asked to serve as acting superintendent for the third time. But when it was time for him to claim a seat with his name on the door and his signature on the contract, he was required to honor a similar request to the one given to Rosa Parks thirty-six years before. Rosa Parks did not honor the request made of her, and neither did T. Y. Lawrence. Both became agents of change because they said "NO!"

There are certain days and places that affect our hearts and minds for the rest of our lives. December 18, 1990, is one of those days for me, and for a lot of folks in Talladega. Prior to that day, Dr. Billy Mills retired as superintendent of schools in Talladega, and Dr. Lawrence was named acting superintendent. I was serving out my third year as president of the board of education. It would prove to be my last year as a member of the board after ten years of service.

The board of education was at that time and remains today a member of the Alabama Association of School Boards (AASB). One service provided by the AASB to its members is guidance and instruction in the search and selection process for a superintendent. The board asked Dr. Lawrence to contact the AASB and arrange a meeting. Responding to the board's request of him, Dr. Lawrence, at the regular June 5, 1990 school board meeting, informed board members that Dr. Sandra Sims-deGraffenried, executive director of the AASB, would meet with the board on June 30, 1990. By that time, Dr. Lawrence had informed the board of his desire to serve the system as its next superintendent.

He asked in the meeting, "Do you want me present at the meeting?"
"Yes," they said.
"Are there special documents that you need?" he asked.
Two members requested brochure information to read.
"I'll have them to you by Monday afternoon."
They thanked him and the meeting was dismissed.

On Saturday, June 30, the board met with Dr. Sims-deGraffenried at the central office. She explained the search procedure, and said that the search could be local, regional, or national. The school board did not have to hire anyone. We were told that we could do it ourselves or have their professional assistance. However, she stated more than five different times in the meeting that the final decision on a superintendent was not a decision of the AASB, but one that had to be made by the Talladega City Board of Education. Every member of the five-person board stated their understanding. Dr. Sims-deGraffenried also stated on more than three occasions in the meeting that after they conducted their search, the board had every right to turn down the top five candidates, ask for all files, or simply start the process over if it wished to do so.

The school board appointed a Citizens Advisory Committee to provide input from the community on the desired qualifications that it felt a superintendent ought to have. The committee was composed of a cross-section of people including parents, teachers, business leaders, politicians, and others. On September 17, 1990, that committee made its report to the school board. Its qualifications were met in every way by Dr. T. Y. Lawrence, our own acting superintendent. Even though the board had approved hiring the AASB to conduct the national search, it was clear to me that our advisory board had described Dr. T. Y. Lawrence in its report.

At that September 17 meeting, I asked that the board reconsider in light of the advisory committee's report. As I saw it, this was our chance to break through old and tired barriers into an intimacy that first and foremost honored loyalty. I further felt that there was no need to spend 5,500 dollars of the school board's money for a search that could and should have ended with the selection of the man who was doing the job.

I informed the board members that I had received numerous calls and contacts from persons throughout the city who felt that it would not demonstrate our best judgment if we proceeded in executing the contract with AASB. Many had said openly that it would not be in the best interest of our city, our children, or our future if we spent more than five thousand dollars to conduct a search that was not necessary.

As of September 17, 1990, the AASB had not begun a search of any kind for our school board because it had not received a signed contract for the services. We had no legal obligation to the AASB, but I felt we did have a moral obligation to listen to the parents of the children we had sworn to serve, and there were hundreds of people who wanted to see this thirty-one-year veteran lead our school system forward. Our advisory committee's report was discussed in place after place in our city. Countless people asked me what was on that list that disqualified Dr. Lawrence, and I told them nothing.

"Then y'all ought to save the money, name him, and move this town forward. Right?" they said.

"I think you're right," I'd reply. "Thanks for sharing your feelings with me." I felt that the people were right. The board, however, voted to enter into contract with the ASSB to conduct the superintendent search, in spite of my objections, at the cost of $5,500. As president of the board, it was my responsibility to execute the contract. I didn't like it, but I did my duty because I had learned the importance of doing so across the years, even when it hurt and was unpleasant. I had found out that Nietzsche was right when he said, "He who would learn to fly one day must learn to stand and walk; one cannot fly into flying."

Days of Conflict

I was shocked and disappointed on that eighteenth day of December, 1990. Just a few days before Christmas, the AASB made their recommendation of five candidates for superintendent to the school board. The recommendation of candidates coupled with the school board's response set in motion a spirit of confrontation and conflict that would last for almost two years. Our small city was catapulted onto the national scene as national wire services picked up this sad story.

The five candidates recommended by the AASB were: Dr. Edison Daniel Barney from Toledo, Ohio, Dr. Jerry R. Hartley from Sank Rapids, Minnesota, Dr. Henry Louis Johnson from Atlantic City, New Jersey, Dr. David Sawyer from Easley, South Carolina, and Dr. Charles W. Townsend from Phoenix, Arizona. The newspaper headline read: "Lawrence Not One of Five Candidates for Superintendent." The article went on:

I was quoted as saying, "As chairman, I am not pleased with either of these candidates. I prefer the AASB board gives us the thirty-seven files of the other candidates and lets us make the determination on this. I don't think this is in the best interest of our children or for moving our system forward."

More than a hundred people gathered for the announcement. The board office was too small to accommodate them. Forty people remained, while the other sixty went to our church to wait. We had all taken for granted that Dr. Lawrence would be named as superintendent. Edythe Sims, a black city-councilwoman, remained. She was outraged and said so. "This is a foolish decision. I urge the board of education to make this matter right. AASB was contracted by the board to do a job. They didn't do a good one, but they don't make the decisions for the school system. The board should add Dr. Lawrence's name to the list. People shouldn't think we are stupid. Nobody, even Dr. Sims-deGraffenried, can explain why Dr. Lawrence isn't a finalist. This whole thing looks like a smokescreen designed to discriminate."

Dr. Sims-deGraffenried emphasized that while three of the five candidates were white, two were black. However, this was quickly interpreted by those blacks present as the old "divide us with us" technique. The two blacks selected would not become superintendent because they had no local support. However, the fact that they were chosen in the top five provided an appearance of fairness. This was only on the surface. The two blacks selected had less than two years central office experience. They would not be able to compete with the three whites, who not only had central office experience, but were working as superintendents. Dr. Lawrence, however, had twenty years of central office experience. It was obvious that the game plan was an insult to the intelligence of thinking people.

One white past elected official was present and said, "It is a reflection on our state. It is a sad day when no one from here is qualified to fill that position. Dr. Lawrence gave his life to this town. He has been chosen to be assistant superintendent and acting superintendent. I don't know how we can turn our backs on this man."

County Commissioner Frank Strickland, the first elected African-American county commissioner member, was present and questioned the AASB's selection, wondering what measuring rod was used. "I can't fathom this. I can't begin to conceive why Dr. Lawrence's name was not among the candidates. Are his qualifications so bad? My mother used to say that we would cut off our nose to spite our face. Are we doing that? We got someone in our own backyard. I hope this board rejects the findings. We've got a gem with Dr. Lawrence in our midst."

While the commissioner was speaking, a thin white woman wearing black-rimmed glasses was sitting in the audience and reportedly said, "Lawrence is not qualified. That's why we don't want him."

Seated two rows behind her was Lillian Lawrence, former Talladega City schoolteacher and wife of Dr. Lawrence. Lillian, with the graciousness that is characteristic of quiet poise and dignity, sat through it all without fear or frowns. Many wondered who the "we" was to whom the woman had referred, and there were suggestions that she was referring to the segregated league group who'd given us so much trouble in the past.

As the talk continued, the mood deepened as each speaker seemed to feel the blow leveled by the report as distinctively personal and deceptively powerful. As he scanned the board room, Eddie Tucker, an articulate black man with a square-shaped face who served as assistant principal at Talladega High School, took the floor, "Dr. Lawrence has done an exemplary job. He works day and night and has been living and dreaming of being superintendent. Are we sending the wrong message to our children? We teach them if they work hard, do the right thing, get the right education and experience, then they have a chance of reaching their dreams. How can we tell them this, when Dr. Lawrence has done just that and he isn't even in the top five. This is a slap in the face. It says it doesn't matter what you do; it doesn't make any difference."

Talladega High School teacher Sharon Anderson, a petite, blond-haired, white female followed Tucker, saying, "I hate this. This is the kind of stuff that keeps giving the South a bad name. I'm very disappointed. The board should nominate Dr. Lawrence. He should be given the chance. If given a chance, he will be the best superintendent this city has had."

Dr. Sims-deGraffenried tried to defend what the AASB had done. "We have thirty-seven strong educators. We were given the task of finding you a superintendent through qualifications set by the Advisory Committee and board. We presented you with five names, which warrant their investigation. The school board will have to hire who they think is best for the boys and girls here. The decision is theirs; let them do their job."

A motion was made. Board member Ray Miller sought to have Dr. Lawrence's name included, but was not successful. No one recommended the motion. It was clear that the vote would have been 3-2. I spoke as board president, saying, "I vehemently oppose this motion."

But they won. Talladega lost. The days would be filled with hostility and the nights would be long. This crisis would ultimately warrant the intervention of Dr. Joseph Lowery, national president of the Southern Christian Leadership Conference.

The Theme of Lies and Slander

Support for Dr. Lawrence was solid. The arguments for his appointment were sound. The group that sought to kill his dream resorted to the age-old "let's tell some lies" technique. On January 1, 1991, the *Talladega Daily Home* newspaper headlines read: "Lawrence's Doctorate in Order, UA Dean Says." Allegations had been raised that there were problems with Dr. Lawrence's doctorate from the University of Alabama in Tuscaloosa. Rumors had been spread claiming that Lawrence either didn't write his dissertation for his doctorate in 1978 or that someone else had written it for him.

The *Daily Home* contacted the University of Alabama regarding Lawrence's doctorate. "As far as we can tell, at this point, everything seems to be in order," said Dr. Ron Rogers, interim dean of the graduate school at UA. "There have been no allegations against Lawrence. In fact, until you called, I hadn't even heard about this."

The rumors were false. They were created and circulated in order to justify the perceived evil that had been done and to destroy the mounting resistance to that evil.

I listened as Dr. Lawrence spoke with eloquence and passion as he addressed the school board and a large gathering of two hundred supporters on a Monday afternoon. "I'm not going to lie to you," he said. "I am disappointed. I have served this system a number of years. I made my home here. I toughed it out through the integration process. I've said to people, 'let's work together.' Let me do my work and let's earn respect. I avoided any confrontation by working behind the scenes. In retrospect, I now wonder if I did the right thing. I have serious questions about the AASB process. What are the qualifications needed to be in the top five? If my experience counts for nothing, then we've got more of a problem here than I thought. I have serious questions about how the school board, the advisory committee, and the search committee operated. Is there some kind of collusion here? I don't see how I wouldn't have met most of the qualifications these five gentlemen have. I've been excluded and I fail to see why. It's mind-boggling to me that my superiors won't give me the job that I'm doing right now. I was the one they asked to contact the AASB and I did it.

"Until this community bands together to resist these entrenched special interest groups, I don't foresee Talladega having the system it ought to have. We must address the needs of all children, with no holds barred. I don't know anyone outside this system who has the experience and knowledge about the Talladega City school system that I do. As Dr. Patterson has said, this is a slap in the face.

"We teach our children that if you live in America, the home of the free and the land of the brave, and you do just things and commit just acts, then you will receive justice. What do you tell that kid from Westgate or Brecon? You tell them to do the right thing, work hard, and see what can be done. I will not apologize for wanting to be treated fairly."

As I listened to Dr. Lawrence, I felt his pain and marveled again at his greatness. By guarding against bitterness, he made it possible for those around him to benefit from his giftedness. I listened to his tone. I watched his physical gestures. I took notice of the content of his words and I admired the way he deliberately avoided using emotionally-charged language in a climate that was jam-packed with strong feelings. Doe was there, but I couldn't look at her. I knew what she must have been feeling and I just couldn't bear to see her pain.

A Time for Action

I was bombarded with calls, conversations, requests, and visits from people throughout Talladega County and beyond. The media was everywhere. I had young people who wanted to fight. I had older people who wanted to curse. I had black people who wanted to strike back with an answer of terror. I had white people who were ashamed of what had been done and fearful of where we were headed. We all wanted to do different things, but we all needed to do one thing. We needed to pray, come together, and respond constructively. I called for a community meeting at our church for the last Sunday night in December of 1990, and 543 people attended that community meeting to discuss ways to respond to the unhappy set of circumstances.

At that meeting, the Talladega Citizens for a Better Society laid the blame on the Talladega City Council, the board of education, and the Junior Welfare League. Talladega County Commissioner Frank Strickland said, "This group of all white females has been controlling education, teacher appointments, and worked behind the scenes to prevent Dr. Lawrence's appointment. They kept Dr. B. E. McKinney from being appointed to the school board. They sell apples using the children of our system to raise money for their Apple Annie Day. They have no black members. They've never had a black member, yet they throw rocks and hide their hands. We want this madness to cease."

Edythe Sims, the fiery city councilwoman, took the floor and said, "We will not and we cannot stand by and see injustice prevail."

Eddie Tucker, with courageous abandon, thundered his opposition to the AASB amid applause after applause. Commissioner Strickland followed Tucker and said, "I've been in Talladega all my life. I know this town. I know the way they work. I've already heard the rumors. They're going to get after Eddie Tucker. We are going to picket those businesses that have ties to all of those folks who pulled this dirty deal. When they go after Tucker, and they will because he is untenured, we'll just throw up some more pickets. It's going to be cold and rainy some days, but we're going to picket anyhow."

Two marches were set on that night. The first march would take place on January 7th at 3 p.m. It would start at Talladega College and proceed to the city hall chambers for the purpose of seeking council intervention. The second march was scheduled for January 15th from Brecon to Salter School to address the board of education at it's regular meeting.

I took the floor at the close of the meeting and stated that this matter would not simply go away. I was aware of the mindset that often permeated the thinking of those steeped in maintaining the status quo. I had seen it often. Some simply beg off issues where strong feelings are involved in the African-American community. They just wait, let things cool off, and go back to business as usual. I warned those in opposition to Dr. Lawrence's dream that it would not go away and die out. I quoted the "black bard," Langston Hughes, who once asked:

> What happens to a dream deferred?
> Does it dry up like a raisin in the sun
> Or fester like a sore and then run.
> Does it stink like rotten meat
> Or crust and sugar over like syrupy sweet
> Or does it explode?

I thanked the people for their presence, prayed, and dismissed them. After the meeting, we had a quick leadership meeting to assess what had happened, make adjustments, and focus on our next steps. We knew that spies had been among us and that they would get the word out quickly.

Eddie Tucker had been the person who first told me that they would send spies to sabotage us, and he was right. We felt that it would have been wrong to take children out of their classes. We would not boycott classes. It would not be consistent with what Dr. Lawrence had done with his life nor with the goals we had for our children.

As long as they didn't know whether we were going to pass or run their defense, they couldn't focus on one thing, but had to be prepared for anything. While they were expecting us to boycott schools, they were getting ready to discredit our protest by attacking us and saying we were using children. We let them prepare for a pass play that would never be called. As long as the spies showed up, we would only discuss issues that we wanted everybody to know about and the strategies that we didn't mind anybody knowing.

On the January 7th march, we'd keep our eyes open for the spies who would have to show up at the starting point at Talladega College, but would not take a chance on making the march to city hall.

A New Revelation

On January 4, 1991, the *Talladega Daily Home* newspaper reported that a letter to the editor was hand-delivered and signed by three Talladega City Board of Education members. On Saturday, the newspaper printed the letter with the headline, "Three School Board Members Issue Statement." In their letter, they had no official minutes, but said these were the facts as they personally recollected them. The letter was signed by the three board members. On the letter, they sought to lay the entire AASB matter in my lap using statements like, "After a full discussion, Reverend Patterson suggested that the board hire AASB" and "Following Reverend Patterson's suggestion, the board requested Dr. Lawrence to place the recommendation for hiring AASB."

Apparently, they had taken some hits. Their attempts to lay the blame on me backfired big time. Forty supporters of Dr. Lawrence had been present when the AASB made its report. Forty supporters had heard me plead with the board to dismiss the AASB, take the thirty-seven files, and move from there. Forty supporters had heard me say, "We have bought something and can't even explain what it is." Forty supporters had watched as school board member Ray Miller sought to have Dr. Lawrence's name added to the list of candidates in vain. Forty supporters had watched those same three school board members vote even as they were asked to remedy the wrong that had been done to Dr. Lawrence. The fact that my pleas fell on deaf ears at that crucial time revealed more about the impact of my influence on the votes of those three board members than any letter could have.

After the article appeared in the newspaper, an even greater ground swell of support erupted for our cause. Several Talladega College fraternity and sorority representatives requested that they be allowed to participate in any way that we deemed appropriate. On the Sunday morning after the newspaper article appeared, seventy-two college students attended our worship service and asked to meet with me after the worship service was concluded.

"Dr. Patterson, we've read the newspaper article. That thing was just another attempt to divide and conquer. Do these people think that we're just that stupid?" asked one petite brown-skinned young woman wearing a green AKA sorority sweater.

One young man by the name of Jason, attired in a navy blue suit, looked at me with tortured eyes, waved the newspaper article, and said, "If they didn't listen to you with forty black folks eyeballing them, then we know whatever they did before, it wasn't because of you or your influence."

"No matter what happens here, we want to be a part of it. We live here nine months out of the year. As students, we spend a lot of money in Talladega. What they did to Dr. Lawrence was wrong. They tell us to get an education, pay our dues, and keep our noses clean. That's what Dr. Lawrence did and we see what happened to him. They'll do the same thing to us wherever we are."

I sat and listened as five others spoke, vented, and pledged themselves to help with the wrong that had been done. As I listened to them speak, I repeatedly told myself that some good would come from this sad set of circumstances.

There were other incidents from the newspaper article released by the three white board members that outraged and mobilized the black community to take action, such as, setting up phone banks to call political leaders, school board members, and other persons perceived as having influence in the community.

In his direct response to the three-member board statement, Commissioner Frank Strickland wrote his insightful letter to the newspaper editor, detailing that there had been new evidence discovered which indicated that the three board members worked to exclude and not fairly consider Dr. T. Y. Lawrence for superintendent of the Talladega City school system. He emphasized that the injustice done to Dr. Lawrence didn't come as a result of the board of education's bad judgment in spending $5,500. This was poor judgment, he admitted, and it did not matter who agreed to hiring the AASB, because it in itself was not the cause of the protest, merely a waste of taxpayers' money. The board should have done the job they were appointed to do and should not have spent taxpayers' money unwisely, he asserted.

The injustice came when the AASB did not name Dr. Lawrence as one of the finalists. Strickland pointed out that a detailed look at the candidates showed that Dr. Lawrence had more qualifications than all the rest.

A second injustice came, Strickland said, when board members as well as citizens questioned the AASB's recommended finalists, but the people and the two dissenting board members were ignored. The board had had previous knowledge that Dr. Lawrence wanted the position, and petitions had been presented on his behalf. He should have been included automatically, because he was a thirty-one-year veteran of the school system and because three thousand signatures had previously been presented on his behalf.

He said that an even greater injustice was being committed because we had a few self-righteous people trying to tell us what was best for the majority. We had the best person for the job in Dr. Lawrence.

During that difficult time, Mr. Clarence Dortch Jr. served as Vice-President of Finances at Talladega College. Strategically located, he and his impressive looking wife, Peggy, provided a monumental service for our city as they counseled young college students who were burning with anger to approach the painful matter within the parameters of reason and wisdom. Reverend Ronnie C. Beavers, Director of Student Affairs at Talladega College and pastor of the First Baptist Church in Pell City, spent long days and weary nights as he rightly intervened to keep the city from going up in smoke.

I was amazed and deeply thankful for the fact that these brilliant people, along with my niece, Floretta James Dortch, an attractive and articulate admissions professional and college counselor, had the influence and used it during that volatile period to curb the potential for violence that permeated the city. The tension, at that time, was as pregnant, with as much a formula for eruption, as any period that I had lived through during the sixties. Strong Christian leaders, like Dr. Samuel Turner, the gifted pastor of the Union Springs Baptist Church, Dr. B. E. McKinney, the Dean of National Baptist pastors in Talladega County and pastor of the Greater Ebenezer Baptist Church, Reverend Clarence Henderson, the splendid pastor of the Shady Grove Baptist Church, Reverend Johnny McKinney, the inspiring pastor of the Rocky Mount Baptist Church and others responsibly kept a bad matter from exploding into a plethora of disaster. Hurting people who do not have proper counsel can become dangerous people. Anger, more often than seldom, is a means of defense.

There is a unique pain that afflicts the soul when the people who wrong you seek to convince you that you've only received what you really deserved. It is from that single actuality that a kinship stronger than blood bonds people to the point that they feel the hurt as a group that is experienced by the individual; where regardless of the person who happens to be the bleeding target for the moment, the group at large suffers with him or her. Dr. Lawrence was the target for the moment. His pain, however, reverberated in the bosom of the masses and the intensity of that reality gave birth to a bitter and ferocious anguish.

As I listened to the spirit of the times, I recalled the wisdom given in my presence, on a day many years before. We were preparing to take on the mean-spirited sheriff of Dallas County in the black belt of Alabama.

Stokely Carmichael, the rising star of a more confrontational movement was furious and wanted to fight over a racial slur that had been hurled at us. Dr. King pulled Stokely aside and said, "Violence only helps our enemies, because it gives them an opportunity to hurt us without carrying the weight of a guilty conscience." I don't know if Stokley or Dr. King took notice of my preoccupation with their exchange, but those words helped form my approach to problem solving.

As we prepared for the inevitable conflict in Talladega, we were fortunate to have joining the ranks of the peace-keepers and counselors Reverend L. L. Jacobs, the impressive pastor of the Kelley Springs Baptist Church, Reverend Jerry Jones, the endearing pastor of the Mount Cleveland Baptist Church, and the Reverend Walter Jones, one of our county's leading pastors living in Talladega, whose priestly duties took him to Auburn several times each week. Through their prayers, preaching, teaching, and counseling, these men of insight, influence, and invincible courage served the cause and prevented our opposition from "hurting us without carrying" what Dr. King called on that day in my presence, "the weight of a guilty conscience."

"As the days be so shall thy strength," was a biblical principle and promise that I found operating in both the physical and spiritual realm. Just as the adrenal glands in the human body pour large amounts of epinephrine into the blood for "fight" or "flight," so was there for me a kind of spiritual empowerment that followed the effort to lay the blame at my door.

Dr. Nathan Cook, pastor—Morning Star Baptist Church, Reverend Freddy Flanningan, pastor—Harper Springs, Reverend Tommy Hardy, pastor—Mount Moriah, Dr. Matthew Leonard, pastor—Antioch, Dr. Stanley Threatt, pastor—New Maryland, Mountain Home and Mount Olive, Dr. William Threatt, pastor—Africa, and my beloved classmate and friend, Reverend Bobby Harris, pastor—The New Hope Baptist Church in Sylacauga and Reverend Henry McGhee—the articulate pastor of the New Hope United Methodist Church all "stormed the gates of heaven" on my behalf. Bobby and his refined wife Brenda made almost daily contact with us and undergirded my spirit as the crisis before me seem to pull me into the center of a massive storm that I could not avoid.

Five Months of Pickets, Marches, Meetings, and Confrontation

On January 7, 1991, under an overcast sky, the first of many marches began and 680 people marched down Battle Street to express their concerns to the Talladega City Council. They overflowed the city chambers. I did not march, but watched from the street. As a member and president of the board of education, my position was clear. My advice had been ignored, but I was still president of the board that could still make things right. As I listened to the words of "We Shall Overcome" fill the air, my soul found new strength to fight the good fight and I prayed that the council would intervene in the role of peacemaker. The city council president allowed several people to speak.

A young black man by the name of André Keith was the first to speak. He approached the speaker's podium, squared his shoulders, and said with perfect diction, "We've come to ask the political leaders to support us in upholding what is right. We are beyond looking at the first black. The people of Talladega have waited patiently for a person like Dr. T. Y. Lawrence who best represents the community as one of our finest. We know that he can be held accountable. There is no person in Talladega or the United States of America who is better qualified than T. Y. Lawrence to direct us through this city's educational storms that we face. This man knows Talladega and he knows the school system's needs.

"Dr. Lawrence has come together with the community not for an argument or confrontation, but to better understand the problems we face in our school system. We must invest in the front side of our students rather than the backside where welfare, reform schools, and prisons are. Dr. Lawrence has served education well in this city, demonstrating a determination to make schooling an instrument of democracy, individual opportunity, and professional and social mobility. One school board member never charged the superintendent, who just retired, with the same charges of inadequacy. Yet, the superintendent is the one who is in charge of the school system. It is also curious that that same board member has not charged those candidates with similar issues in the school system from which they are now working. You and I both know that such charges are not only irresponsible, but they are ridiculous. We will know by your actions today whether you govern all the people of this city."

Josie Thomas, a retired black educator with large eyes who served as chairwoman of the powerful Talladega County Democratic Conference, made her way to the speaker's stand. She encouraged the council to sign a resolution asking that all boards in the city consider hiring local, qualified people first. She also asked the council to endorse a letter to the Talladega Board of Education seeking the appointment of Dr. Lawrence as school superintendent.

"You, as city government leaders, appoint all city board members," she said. The board of education membership has been appointed by this council. You had an opportunity to appoint Dr. B. E. McKinney to this board only a few months ago. We asked you to do so. His appointment would have given us two African-Americans on the board that oversees a school system that is, at a minimum, 45 percent black. It is sad, but the teaching population is only 18 percent black. We know that the school board has disrespected Dr. Lawrence. An injustice has taken place. You are responsible for this evil monster that seeks to destroy the racial unity and progressive spirit of this community. I respectfully ask that you intervene and use your influence creatively and productively."

Commissioner Frank Strickland: "I stand before you with a lot of hope in my heart. This is an issue of right and wrong. Injustice takes away a man's hope. It destroys hope and there is very little reason to continue when hope is gone. Injustice anywhere, as Dr. King once said, is a threat to justice everywhere. Don't let a few people divide this town. Go on record with us. Let's live and work together."

Eddie Tucker, the articulate and passionate spokesperson for the Citizens Coalition called for a united response from government leaders and spoke eloquently about the issues at hand.

After patiently standing during the formal presentation, Mr. Lawrence McGraw and his wife Maenola, both career educators who had marched and inspired countless people, spoke forcefully and personally to each council person who would listen. They summoned individual members to be ruled by the best hope for the future rather than bow to the pressure to repeat the mistakes of the past.

Johnny Harris and his wife Laura, also educators midway in their careers, thrust themselves into the center of the controversy and sought to solicit council intervention.

Doe, Horace Jr., and Jay marched and their presence buoyed me as I wearily edged my way through the mazes and pitfalls that seemed to swell with each rejection.

The council refused to support the Lawrence appointment, but adopted a policy for hiring locals. The pickets, marches, meetings, and debates went on as the school board interviewed candidates. One candidate, Dr. David Sawyer of Easley, South Carolina, withdrew. The four others were interviewed, and with a three-to-two vote, Dr. Edison Daniel Barney of Toledo, Ohio was selected. He accepted the job and remained in it for less than two years, leaving Talladega to accept another superintendent position in another Alabama town.

Retaliated Against, But Victorious

John Carzello once said, "Courage is having the strength to shape the world when it's easier to let somebody else do it for us."

The rumors were flowing everywhere. My days on the school board were numbered. My appointment would end May 1, 1991 if I were not reappointed. It was 3:30 in the afternoon on April first, the day of the city council meeting when my appointment would come up. The phone rang, and I answered it.

The voice said triumphantly, "You don't stand a dog's chance in hell to be re-appointed."

I answered, resigned to the inevitable, "You're probably right," and hung up.

The vote was three to two; I lost. As always, Doe was right there. When the word came in, she held my hand and asked, "Are you all right?"

"Yes. I expected it."

"I did too. What are you going to do?"

I said, "I have four of the best-looking steaks that they had at Winn Dixie and I've got some charcoal."

"Silly, I'm not talking about dinner," Doe said.

"I know, but I am. Let's just do this together. The kids will love it. Tomorrow is another day. Things will work out."

As I fired up the grill, Dr. Lawrence called. "I'm sorry," he said.

"I know. Don't worry. It's turning out just as we thought it would. Have you made contact?"

"Yes," he said. I spoke with the lawyers last week."

"Good! We are about to move into phase two. God help us. I'd hoped that it would not have to come to this."

As long as the board interviewed, talked, and made no decision to employ a superintendent other than Dr. Lawrence, no laws were broken. It was wrong. It was mean-spirited, but it was not illegal until such time as the new superintendent was employed. As for me, it was time to make lemonade because the city council had given me the lemons.

My political enemies were rejoicing. My phone rang often with unidentified, jubilant, sarcastic callers making a host of statements such as, "You're dead in this town," "Sooner or later folk like you get cut down to size," and "I'm just glad I'm around to see it." I said nothing, hung up the phone, and girded myself to the test ahead.

Many members and friends also called with words of encouragement. I received a lot of inspiring cards. Occasionally, I would run into some who were curious about my future. Several political groups circulated questionnaires and leaflets to test the political waters concerning a mayoral bid on my behalf. Two city councilmen openly boasted that I had been replaced because of my support for Dr. Lawrence. I prayed and gave serious thought to my words before I granted interviews with the media. After a few days, I began to grant interviews.

On the issue of the council's decision not to reappoint me, I answered, "It's no tragedy that I wasn't reappointed. It would be a tragedy if I felt strongly about something and I was afraid to verbalize my convictions. That would have been a real tragedy.

"A great thing happened before the eyes of this community, when this escalated to the protest marches. Many said Talladega would be like another southern town where children would be kept out of school. We didn't do that. We continued to have school and at no time did our people use children. That's something that should make us all proud. We had people on both sides who were responsible and did not stoop to using children to protest some point. The administrators, faculties, and support personnel continued to have school and educate children. I apologize for not making their jobs easy during these past five months. I hate that this matter was not solved in a more amicable manner. I continue to be impressed by the professional demeanor of Dr. Lawrence as he continued to keep before us the most important fact—children. He never lost focus!"

When questioned about the kind of message the controversy sent, I answered, "I hope the message is not representative of Talladega because it paints us as a warmed-over version of the Old South, rather than being a progressive member of the New South. As our soldiers are returning from painting the sands of the Middle East with their blood and we are waving American flags in celebration, are we saying you are going to be penalized if you say something that some don't agree with? I believe in what we are told about the greatness of America. But in 1991, are you still going to be penalized because you are black? This erodes our ability to be one as a nation. I knew what could happen. It's political knee-capping, which may be as American as apple pie, but it's not right and it doesn't provide an environment where you get the best ideas. While race was a factor, it's really a matter of right and wrong. One of the men on the Alabama Association of School Boards' search committee was black and two of the candidates were black.

"I'm proud to live in Talladega, but I am not proud to have been a part of a board that dealt unfairly with an honorable man. I was embarrassed. We are not painting the best picture for this town that is pregnant with rich opportunities. City officials encourage the public to shop locally and spend dollars at home, but I think we sent a dangerous message to our young administrators in the school system. I wish the board well, but its future will be cloudy if it fails to communicate respect to local personnel.

"After spending ten years on the school board, I am convinced that we've got to increase local funding. Local dollars are important because they reveal the worth that the local community places on education. What happens in the classroom has a direct relationship with what happens at the Chamber of Commerce. We've got to do a better job of funding education, and I don't mean with quick fixes that promise a lot and deliver little. There is no painless cure to remedy the ills that assault public education."

On Sunday, April 7th, the local newspaper printed an editorial wishing me well and thanking me. They also said my public service was far from over.

At its first meeting in May, the board of education presented me with a plaque for my ten years of service. A number of people were thrilled to see me go. I was no longer a board member, but I was far from being gone. Ralph Waldo Emerson once said, "If you shoot at a king, you must kill him." I was not a king. I had been shot and hit, but I was not dead.

The Alabama Dream Team

I first began to discuss legal action against the Talladega City Council a week after I was replaced on the board of education. Living in a small town like Talladega teaches you to keep your mouth shut until your ducks are in a row. The attorneys handling Dr. Lawrence's case were some of the best education, voting rights, and civil rights lawyers in the nation. Each was famous and a legend in his own time. These white guys were the "Dream Team" long before the phrase was coined—John C. Falkenberry, Edward Still, Joe Whatley, James U. Blacksher of Birmingham and Reo Kirkland, Jr. of Brewton. They were working on Dr. Lawrence's lawsuit and after a good deal of prayer and discussion, I joined the lawsuit that would be filed in the U. S. District Court for the Northern District of Alabama.

The word was getting around in the community that since I was off the board, the board would go after every leader involved in the Lawrence controversy that was employed with the city school system. The mentality was that it was time to teach them all a lesson.

As the days moved on, the spirit of the Bourbons, that mindset that pitted blacks and whites against one another for the personal gain and pleasure of a power-crazed minority was prevalent.

Reportedly, the group had mounted an assault on the local newspaper in general and Denise Sinclair, the white reporter who covered the controversy, in particular. Ms. Sinclair eventually accepted the Sylacauga beat, which is twenty miles from the city of Talladega. She had reported the story with integrity and some people hated her for it.

One afternoon, as I discussed the matter in my home with several members of our legal team, my daughter, Ivy, overheard some of our conversation. After my guests left our home, Ivy looked up at me and said, "Daddy, I knew that you were going to fight them. I love you." I reached down and picked her up and she kissed me on the cheek. With a lump in my throat, I said, "I didn't know that you paid any attention to this kind of stuff. I love you too."

"Daddy, I know they tried to hurt you and that makes me mad," she replied as her dancing eyes seemed to glow with a fresh brightness and insight that is uncommon in a four year old.

As Ivy and I sat in the den, I basked in the warmth of a daughter's love and, for a while, the legal issues grew dim in importance.

There are a lot of things that I don't understand. For instance, how do gazelles survive when they don't drink water? I am told that somehow through their chemical process, solid food provides them with all the moisture that they need. I don't understand why, if Denny's restaurants are open every day of the year, twenty-four hours a day, why they put locks on the door. I still don't understand how, when, or the way everything happened, but our opposition created the climate for an ideal federal lawsuit that would change the selection process for all school board members in the future of the city of Talladega.

During the months of April and May, both Dr. Lawrence and I worked quietly, met clandestinely, and communicated often with the various members of our legal team. It was hard to keep quiet. Supporters often called or stopped me, saying, "It's just not right." The opposition had penalized Dr. Lawrence. They had replaced me, but they had not put the fire out. We kept quiet. We kept working.

Winston Churchill once said to his nation, "I have nothing to offer but blood, toil, tears, and sweat." He also said, "I have never accepted what many people have kindly said, namely that I have inspired the nation. It was the nation and the race dwelling all around the globe that had the lion heart. I had the good fortune to be called upon to give the roar." I knew that we were working on something very special. It was one of those unique times when providence gives you a chance to affect your world beyond your grave. While they did not give interviews to the newspaper, I knew that we were dealing with some very powerful people and a very powerful force. It was the force of intimidation, the kind that makes people afraid without them knowing that they are afraid.

In June of 1991, our federal lawsuit was filed. It involved both the Talladega City Board of Education and the Talladega City Council. Dr. Lawrence filed legal action against the board of education for back pay, front pay, and the present value of an annuity to compensate for the difference between the pension he would receive from the Alabama Teacher Retirement system and the pension that he would have received had he been promoted to superintendent and served in that capacity for one year.

It was not about money. It was not about revenge. Dr. Lawrence later said, "I was not out to get somebody or thought I was better than anyone else. I just wanted to be treated with decency and respect. I never had any poor evaluations to my knowledge and I had always done what was expected of me.

"I was frustrated and disappointed to know I couldn't apply or even be allowed on the playing field. It was like working in a place for a long, long time and realizing that you can't reach your goal because of your race. It was my turn at bat. They enlarged the strike zone and moved the fence back. It was wrong. It should not have happened to anybody. I hope that it never happens again. All people, regardless of gender or race, ought to be treated with decency and respect."

My legal action was aimed directly at changing the appointment method of selecting school board members to that of electing them. I alleged that I was not reappointed to the school board because of my support for Dr. Lawrence's candidacy. The opposition had given tons of statements saying this was the case. I am certain that had they known the lawsuit was coming, they would have been far less verbal with public statements.

My action also alleged that the appointment method of selecting members of the Talladega City Board of Education violated Section 2 of the Voting Rights Act of 1965, as amended, by diluting the voting strength of black people and denying citizens equal access to the political processes of governance in the Talladega City public school system.

The rumors of further retaliation became fact. The school board violated the state law and did not renew several employees who were involved in the support of Dr. Lawrence. Their action was illegal because in the state of Alabama, a school board has to have a superintendent's recommendation to hire, terminate, or non-renew employees. Dr. Lawrence was still acting superintendent at that time and refused to recommend that those protest leaders be non-renewed. The school board ignored his unwillingness to do so and even spent several hundred dollars for research on tenured employees. This was, we perceived, done with the goal of terminating other employees such as my wife, Doe, who was at that time a tenured middle school principal.

Three people that the opposition desperately wanted to fire were Eddie Tucker, Julius Thomas, and Katrina Buchanan. These three black people had been courageous and consistent in their open support for Dr. Lawrence. They were nontenured and therefore considered to be vulnerable.

In order to reduce the school system's financial obligations in the wake of state proration, Dr. Lawrence recommended non-renewal contracts of all teachers hired in 1989 and 1990. Dr. Lawrence specifically did not recommend nonrenewal of teachers hired in 1988 because there was no financial need to do so. While these three people were untenured, they had also been hired in 1988. The white majority of the board of education overrode Dr. Lawrence's recommendation and non-renewed the contracts of all teachers hired in 1988 as well. The purpose of the board's action in non-renewing the contracts of all teachers hired in 1988 was to dismiss black teachers who supported Dr. Lawrence for superintendent—in particular, Eddie Tucker, Katrina Buchanan, and Julius Thomas. This would, in their eyes, intimidate all black employees of the Talladega City school system who would dare to speak up for racial equality and fairness.

In a matter of days these three protest leaders, along with several other employees, contacted our legal team and joined in a motion to intervene and to seek a preliminary injunction against the school board for its illegal action. They asked the court to enter a preliminary injunction requiring the reinstatement of petitioners and the class of nontenured teachers whose contracts were illegally non-renewed without the recommendation of the acting superintendent. The class of '88, as we eventually named them, had a strong enough case to have prevailed on the merits of their state law claims.

The school board's notification of non-tenured teachers hired in 1988 that their contracts would not be renewed was strictly illegal, because the acting superintendent, Dr. T. Y. Lawrence, refused to recommend such nonrenewal. To have become legally effective, notification required both the recommendation of the superintendent and the approval of the governing board.

The legal team argued forcefully that the public interest required issuance of the preliminary injunction. They stated that Alabama law protected teachers from that kind of arbitrary and capricious action. They said that the public interest would suffer if the law was frustrated and ignored with impunity.

They were right. Dr. King was right—"Injustice anywhere is a threat to justice everywhere." If a school board could frustrate the law in Talladega to intimidate African-Americans, a large corporation could do the same in Texas to overlook females, Hispanics, Catholics, or anybody who is different from the majority. They asked for three responses from the federal court: to schedule a speedy hearing to allow the parties to present such evidence as may be necessary to determine whether the preliminary injunction should be issued, to certify a plaintiff–intervenor class of all teachers illegally notified that their contracts were not being renewed, and to enter a preliminary injunction requiring the school board to immediately reinstate Tucker, Buchanan, Thomas, and all members of the class they represented in the positions they were assigned under their 1990-1991 contracts, along with all salary and benefits that they would have received if not for the illegal action of the defendant board.

The day of the hearing arrived. It was a hot morning. I had not slept well the night before. I had chased sleep in vain even as I assured myself that things would go well. I don't know if it was worry or simple anticipation, but the night seemed so long.

The hearing was scheduled in Gadsden, a forty-five-minute drive from Talladega. Doe and I chatted as I drove toward the federal courthouse. A large group of supporters followed. Many remained behind and prayed. Their prayers worked. Our attorneys were brilliant. I testified for our side for about thirty minutes. I braced myself for cross-examination, but they had no questions for me.

When I returned to my seat beside Doe, she gripped my hand and said, "The law and the truth is on our side. You did great."

I breathed a sigh of relief. "I hope so."

Dr. Lawrence and Eddie Tucker both testified to the specifics. The morning wore on and the judge informed us that he would respond within days.

On July 31, 1991, the court entered a preliminary injunction ordering the immediate reinstatement of Tucker, Buchanan, and Thomas.

City Councilman, Horace Patterson

Instead of running for mayor, I decided to run for the city council position in my ward. The incumbent did not seek reelection. I had two opponents. The lawsuit had further created another group of detractors for me. Thankfully, it had also generated a sense of excitement among well-wishers and supporters.

I didn't take anything for granted. I knew that some big bucks would be spent to defeat me. The money flowed. Some who took it told me, "Hey, I'm getting paid to work against you. I'm going to play the game, but you got my vote."

My nephew, Sylvester James, whom we referred to as Sly, worked like a Trojan among the young voters. Sly, at that time, was coaching both football and basketball. He spent a lot of time during those summer months raining down three-point shots and talking about the importance of my election to the city council.

My church members were wonderful and so were my many friends. Sometimes it takes a crisis to bring a mixed blessing into your life because it has a tendency to separate the wolves from the sheep. It is always a mistake to complain about your woes because it only discredits you. Problems pass, but people remember. My supporters stood out for their courage, adaptability, and stamina.

Clarence McKenzie, a clean-shaven, brown-skinned man, and his lovely and insightful wife Nellie, who was a woman of great influence, worked both night and day identifying my supporters.

Fannie Mae Phillips is an elderly woman with an oval face. To this day, I affectionately call her "Mama Fannie." She always seemed to know the exact time to simply call and say, "I love you. You are my special son and God has a special work for you to perform." Her voice calmed me and gave me strength on the days when I would look downward at my hands and feel that the task of lifting them required more energy than I could summon.

Daisy Cochran, a young woman whose smiling face seemed to remove the shadows of low hanging clouds, transferred my campaign literature into Braille for the visually impaired.

Mary Lou Brown, a thin, energetic, and youthful woman seemed to know all the right strings to pull. She walked the talk of commitment as she registered voters and helped to educate them on real empowerment.

Marie Player, a light-skinned woman with light brown eyes helped to motivate and organize our telephone bank.

Thomas Pugh, a tall, muscular, black man with a receding hairline served as deacon along with Mr. Willie Farrior at the Greater Ebenezer Baptist Church. They both guided me as we developed a platform to address the needs of the large blind and visually impaired population in the voting district.

The black husband-and-wife teams of Sylvester and Peggy Garner, Harold and Jan Foster, James and Barbara Storey, George and Katrina Buchanan, Louis and Sadie Clark, Ed and Annette Reaves, Columbus and Ludie Young, Wilby and Hattie Wallace, Rev. Marshall and Vivian Hawkins, Eddie and Meriam Tucker, Jerome and Hazel Jackson, Harold and Deneen Draper, Johnny and Rose Lawler, Monroe and Shirley Allen, Lawrence and Maenola McGraw, and Horace and Shirley Sims all sought with success to recruit new workers as we found ourselves facing the deep pockets of the new age Bourbons who employed the old age tactics of divide and conquer as taught by Willie Lynch.

One Thursday afternoon amid the rattle of campaign buttons, flyers, and papers, Wren Calhoun, Jr. called and asked to see me. Wren is a man of average size with quick wit. He spoke quickly as I arrived. "How is your campaign going?" he asked.

With one fluid motion I lifted my eyes and shook his hand replying, "I think that we are doing well. What do you think?"

"You're looking good, but you've got to keep working hard. You can't lighten up."

"Yes, I know," I replied as I sat down in a comfortable chair in his den. I listened to the issues that he defined as significant, which included police presence and protection, along with street improvements. As I listened to him speak, I became keenly conscious of his desire to lift the city and considered myself fortunate to garner his support.

The prayers of strong motherly women in our church like Mary Nix, Lillie Bledsoe, Annie Castleberry, Ossie Baker, Emma Peasant, Mary Garret, Jo Ann Turner, Catherine Curry, Minnie Johnson, Louise James, Francis Orr, Martha Pinkston, Bobbie Wiggins, and Ella Canady kept our work on track. This was of unmeasured value because people driven by ambition, regardless of how worthy, sometimes succeed outwardly only to fail inwardly. These wonderful women, paraphrasing Milton, "also served as they stood and waited" and our outer resources multiplied but not at the cost of our spiritual energy. Regardless of the evil assaults, we never felt the feeling of hopelessness engulfing us even as we knew that there were some pockets of opposition that we could not convert.

Then it happened. I saw something that summer that turned my stomach. The detractors had tried filth and it had not worked. This time they paid people to advance an even sicker argument. It was an argument that tried to create church jealously—5,000 dollars was spent during that summer trying to develop a "We Hate Mt. Canaan" movement. The fact that this approach was taken informed me just how desperate my detractors had become.

A local pastor came by to see me. He was a portly built black man with darting eyes. "Dr. Patterson, there are some things being said that you need to know about."

"Thank you. Please tell me."

"There are some folks saying that we should vote against you because your church has too much influence in this city," he said.

"What do you think?"

"I think it's a sign that we've got some pretty little people in our city and there are some who are scared to death that you're going to win this election."

"Will you help me?" I asked.

"That's why I'm here. You are my brother and I respect the ministry that God has given you."

We talked for a while longer and he left inspired. I left the house and moved through the community. They had done some damage, but nothing was beyond repair.

I had a terrific group of volunteer workers whose ranks continued to swell as a result of intervention from my niece Floretta James Dortch, a young mother of two beautiful children and her husband, attorney Clarence Dortch. Both were graduates of Talladega College.

Betty Fleming, a pecan-skinned soft-spoken member of our church, Sharon Curry, a tall young woman with a pear-shaped face, Myrtis Curry, the lovely sister of Sharon, Myrtle Fuller, a bright spirited woman with deep political convictions, Maude Swain, a woman of great beauty and cognizance, Margaret Davis, affectionately nick-named Jue-Baby, Hattie Patterson, the sightly leader of our nurses guild, Emily Jenkins, a petite and articulate woman of great courage and integrity and her husband, Terran, a soft-spoken man whose love for the beloved community has grown by leaps and bounds, all worked to push back the tide created by the flow of the Judas circle who'd taken the 5,000 dollars to defeat me.

Walter Moore, an Air-Force veteran like myself, and his brother-in-law, John Colley, along with Lester Rowls and Percy Cotton each seemed to market me as a man who would exceed the requirements of the council seat and would become a star for others to follow. In the presence of such support one is not bold to speak, but simply appreciative.

There is an African (Swahili) proverb that says, "Don't jump in a fight if you have no weapons." That was not the case with us. On my side was Carol Garrett, a velvety-voiced soloist, Cora Green, a beautiful woman with colorful mannerisms, Rosa Curry, a radiant mother-hearted public educator, and Annette Coleman, a self-motivated rosy-cheeked woman who seemed to mirror the old Portuguese saying that "whomever is well prepared has won the battle." Each woman stood their ground and helped me to stand mine because of their commitment to our common vision for the future of our church and our community.

Our work appeared to be fruitful, but I took nothing for granted. I knew that Sophocles was right when he wrote, "One must wait until the evening to see how splendid the day has been." My enemies' rage intensified. I remembered the profound words of Dietrich Bonhoeffer as he said, "We must form our estimate of men less from their achievements and failures and more from their sufferings."

One of our gifted teachers was Dale Moore, a petite, graceful, and awe-inspiring woman. As she stood before her adult women Sunday school class she shared an insightful dialogue with her sister, Bobbye Thompson and concluded it with the words of Charles Haddon Spurgeon, "God is too good to be unkind and too wise to be confused. If I cannot trace his hand, I can always trust his heart."

I am amazed at how often I have found myself in the right place at the right time. It cannot be luck. I am convinced that it is providence. One beloved member of my parish, Stanley Rembert, calls it "being kept by hands you can't see."

A lady of resplendent beauty, Susie Sykes, defines it as "living on a level where the wolves can't destroy you" and Lavonne Fails, an imposing and majestic-looking woman wise beyond her years calls it "the outcome of overcoming."

A man of sturdy moral fiber with a robust outlook by the name of Willie Canady calls it "being blessed sometimes, even in spite of yourself and having a table prepared for you in the presence of your enemies."

A woman with a heart of gold, Alma Cooper, often smiling with a glint of excitement in her eyes, defines it as "the results of staying where you've been planted."

Deacon Roy Wiggins, an elderly stately looking man of salt-and-pepper hair with a voice that seems to calm even the most tempestuous scenes, calls that unique state "the results of taking care of your field, because if you take care of your field, your field will take care of you."

Patricia Scales and her sweet-spirited sister, Juanita Truss, seem to capture the essences of that special moment by saying, "There comes a time when everybody seems to get a little bit of what's coming to them."

Gerald Douglas, a tall, muscular, education administrator, and his dazzling wife, Charon, have on more than one occasion expressed their belief system in the Danish proverb that "Envy does not enter an empty house," meaning that success never arrives without regret, but in spite of the regret it arrives.

Henry Ashley, a man who sports a well trimmed raven beard and speaks with insight that is peculiar to one who has seen good prevail in spite of the untiring energy of evil, encouraged me as he spoke of a Tibetan proverb which says, "If the heart be stout, a mouse can lift an elephant."

Simpson Bolden, Jr., a well dressed, smooth talking, confident man and his sweet wife Yvonne hoisted my expectations as they referred "to the special hour of victory that comes because the element of goodness is always irresistibly at work."

Alberta Beavers, an impressive-looking woman with compassionate eyes, heightened my confidence as she spoke of that singular time, "as a time when the old has to give way to the new, because once the dawn has started nobody can stop it."

Deacon Wiley Lucas, a man of imposing size with an athletic history that once included being drafted by the National Football League, and his resplendent wife Faye, call this exclusive time, "the earned threshold of an exciting new era of development regardless of those who seek to prevent it."

Robert Tubbs, a slender-built man of brown skin with exceptional golfing skills and his wife Patricia, whose voice as a soloist in our church is truly anointed, views that time as the hour in which the old Chinese proverb comes true which says, "If the string is long enough, the kite will always fly high."

J. D. Houston and his remarkable wife Daisy defines such a time as, "A kiss from heaven blown from the hands of God."

Felicia Walker, a bright-eyed, exquisite-looking, and tenderhearted woman perceives this time as, "The reward that is given with caution and kept with care."

Doe took charge as my campaign manager and as my most loyal supporter. Horace Jr., Jay, and Ivy worked in our door to door campaign. Whenever I felt weary, they inspired me to work harder.

We took the time to talk, ask questions as well as answer them, and work hard, and before the summer of 1991 ended, I became the city councilman elect from Ward I.

It was unique and sweet. The very body that had failed to reappoint me was soon to find me as a part of it. I knew that some would see my election as some kind of formula for revenge. I knew better. I knew that it had to be about more profound issues, so I watched my heart and my words very carefully. I remembered Edmund Morrison's words: "Like stones, words are laborious and unforgiving, and the fitting of them together, like the fitting of stones, demands great patience and strength of purpose and particular skill." I knew that my strength would last only as long as I kept my heart attached to my sense of purpose.

I had been given a great opportunity. It had come dressed in adversity, but it had come. It had come through sorrow and public humiliation, yet it had come. It had come even as a result of deeds done to harm me, yet I had been given a great opportunity. It is said that a grapefruit is a lemon that saw a chance to grow and took it. My election to the city council was my chance to keep growing, and I approached it in that manner.

Frank Curry, a member of our parish and long time businessman, and his graceful wife Sadie, a retired science teacher who taught all three of my children, sent me a lovely card which appealed to my higher self. The card quoted Helen Keller who said, "The best and most beautiful things in the world cannot be seen or even touched. They must be felt with the heart."

The Settlement of the Lawsuit

The court decree was issued with the consent of all parties, without a trial of any contested issues. The school board agreed to the entry of the decree to, as they said, "demonstrate good faith and to avoid the risks, burdens, and expense of continued litigation, and to promote full enforcement of federal civil rights and voting rights laws." The city council, upon which I then sat, agreed to the terms that created an elected school board.

It was ordered, adjudged, and decreed that the school board would pay Dr. T. Y. Lawrence back pay, front pay, and the value of an annuity to compensate him for the difference between his pension and the pension that he would have received if he had been named superintendent, that the preliminary injunctions entered in favor of the Class of '88 were permanent, and that the school board would reinstate Katrina Buchanan in the position of second grade teacher at Houston Elementary School at the beginning of the next school semester.

The defendants would take no adverse action whatsoever against plaintiffs and plaintiffs-intervenors in retaliation for their participation in this action or for their participation in events which were the subject of this action. Within sixty days from the effective date of this order, the defendant City of Talladega would adopt, by ordinance or resolution, a single-member district plan for electing the five members of the Talladega City Board of Education. The said plan would be based on the 1990 federal decennial census, would include the location of all polling places, and would meet all requirements of federal and state law, including the requirements of the fourteenth amendment to the Constitution of the United States and the Voting Rights Act of 1965, as amended. There would be at least one polling place in each school board district. The single-member district plan for the school board would be identical to the plan used for the election of members of the Talladega City Council at its next election.

Within thirty days from the date of its adoption, the defendant City of Talladega would submit for pre-clearance under Section 5 of the Voting Rights Act, 42 U.S.C. section 1973b the single-member district plan and all related changes of laws, ordinances, resolutions, or regulations necessary for the conduct of elections for members of the Talladega City Board of Education. If the plan and related changes were denied Section 5 pre-clearance, the defendant City of Talladega would act promptly to correct the problems identified in the pre-clearance process and would promptly submit a new or modified plan for pre-clearance.

Within ten days from the date the election plan would be pre-cleared under Section 5 of the Voting Rights Act, the plan would be submitted to the court for final appearance.

Following the final approval of a single-member district plan by the court, elections for all five seats on the Talladega City Board of Education would be held on a nonpartisan basis. The school board members elected would serve until successors were elected at the next regular school board elections, which would be held at the same time as regular elections for the Talladega City Council. Thereafter, school board members would serve terms of four years.

Within thirty days from the date the plan was finally approved by the court, the defendant City of Talladega would carry out the responsibility of assigning all qualified voters in the City of Talladega to their school board districts and would inform voters by mail and/or by publishing in the local newspaper a voter list showing the school board districts they resided in and where their polling places were. The location of the new polling places would be determined after consultation with members of the black community. Black citizens would be appointed as poll officials in numbers that reasonably reflected the racial compositions of the districts.

The qualifying period for filing declarations of candidacy for the school board would be set according to Alabama law for regular or special municipal elections, as applicable. All candidates for the school board would be qualified electors of the City of Talladega and the school board district in which they resided.

With the stroke of Federal Judge U. W. Clemons, a new era began in the city of Talladega. The judge gave a gag order to prevent the detailed disclosure of Dr. Lawrence's settlement. He also provided that the chairmanship of the board rotate equally among the five members during their terms. On September 1, 1991, Dr. Lawrence retired from the school system and took the job as chairman of the Education Department at Talladega College.

In February of 1993, Dr. T. Y. Lawrence ran for a seat in the first school board elections in the city of Talladega. He had opposition. This was nothing new. He won. He was then seated and eventually served as president of a school board that had at one time shunned him.

After his election to the school board, Dr. Lawrence was given the opportunity to, of all things, participate in the selection of a new superintendent. Dr. Edison Barney resigned to take another superintendent position after an explosive period involving an issue of students being strip-searched.

The parents of two black girls claimed that their daughters were made to go into the bathroom and strip off all of their clothing in order to be searched. A white girl had claimed that someone had stolen some money from her. Even though the girls who were searched claimed to have been innocent, they were directed, according to their account, to undergo the humiliating ordeal. No money was found on them even though they were stripped and searched.

With quiet determination, the school board conducted a local search. This time they employed a local white male who had given years of service to the city school system. He did not have the academic credentials nor the years of central office experience that the board had overlooked in Dr. Lawrence's case, but he had served. He was chosen. He had dreamed of being superintendent. His dream came true and the man whose dream had been dashed had the class to help make it happen.

Maybe that's a test that God gives us all. He watches to see what we do with the bad stuff that happens to us, because he lets it happen in order to help us make somebody else's dream come true. And maybe, just maybe, as we help to make others' dreams come true, we graduate from being dreamers to dream-makers.

It's hard, but it's not impossible to help seat others in the places that have been denied to you, if that is what you're supposed to do. The cycle of pain has to stop somewhere. It is a special compliment paid to the man or woman who is made strong enough to become a breaker of pain and all that it does to the human spirit. Who is the greater person? Is it the one who rules or the one who serves? Is it the people who hate or the people who know the cost of hate and determine that the cost is too high? Is it the pain-maker or the pain-breaker? Is it the man who walks on others just because he can or the man who has been walked on and works with his whole heart to make himself the last person to know what that experience feels like? Is it the heartbreaker who rejoices in his cruelty or is it the heartbroken who empathizes with a compassion that was gathered from the places of his heart breaks? Is it the person who pushes others into the dark or is it the person who, after having been in the dark, seeks to turn on a light that will keep others from stumbling in places that are both dangerous and deadly? Is it the person who keeps doing wrong because that's the way it has always been done or is it the person who seeks to do right even if it has never been done before? Is it the man who makes news because of the pain he causes or is it the man who makes history because of the help he gives?

After the local superintendent retired, the school board once again contracted with the Alabama Association of School Boards to do a national search. This time they simply requested that all local qualified school employees be included in the number of persons submitted as candidates. Two local employees were submitted and interviewed. One candidate was Dr. Dolia McIntosh Patterson—Doe—principal of Houston Elementary School. She was not selected, but she was given a courtesy denied to Dr. Lawrence. An elected school board made its selection without the assistance of Dr. Lawrence. At the time of that decision-making, Dr. Lawrence had relocated to live with God. Walter Lippmann once said, "The final test of a leader is that he leaves behind in other men the conviction and the will to carry on."

The conviction and the will to carry on permeates a city that learned a hard lesson the hard way. Talladega used its mistakes as stepping stones and began to love itself, not just for the city that it was, but also for the community that it could become by embracing all of its sons and daughters.

One of the city councilmen that voted against my reappointment to the school board had been reelected. We did not speak to one another after he cast his vote until we were sworn in as a new governing body in October of 1991. Prior to the school board issue, we had enjoyed a common commitment. However, neither of us was certain that we could appraise the damage done to our former relationship with accuracy, so we each kept our distance.

In late September, two weeks prior to my formal entry into the council seat, Doe, the kids, and myself took a brief trip to Mobile. As we walked among the floral wonderland of Bellingrath Gardens, Doe said, "Honey, do you think that you're going to be able to work with him?"

"I'm sure that we will. What's that old saying about we'd better hang together or we will surely hang separately?"

"Now don't get historical and philosophical with me," she said. "I really hope that you guys will find a way to heal the city."

Just then, Horace and Jay ran up to us, laughing intensely. I asked, "What's up with you two?"

Jay answered, "Dad, we've got a good one for you. Tell me, why did the chicken cross the road?"

I answered, "That's tired. I remember that answer from when I was a kid. The chicken crossed the road to get to the other side."

Jay, still laughing almost uncontrollably, answered, "Wrong! Tell him, Horace!"

Horace answered, "The chicken crossed the road because he saw two brothers following him with a biscuit."

I joined the laughter. "That was a smart chicken," I said as we then sat together as a family in the breathtaking Oriental-American Garden that had originally served as a drainage area for a free-flowing Artesian well. In that quiet and tranquil climate, we sat for a while without speaking. There is something about the beauty of a world steeped in the blooming and blossoming splendor of red, yellow, white, green, and pink petals decked with swans, Canadian geese, birds, and ducks that is beyond words. You just behold it with wonder.

Doe passed me the postcard that she had purchased in the gift shop. It was a card that pictured the Bellingrath Gardens when the tulips were blooming. While the picture was captivating, the epitaph written by Walter Bellingrath in honor of his wife's memory was even more so:

Bessie Morse Bellingrath
1878—1943
I shall always think of you
wandering through a lovely garden,
like that which you fashioned
with your own hands, where flowers
never fade and no cold wind of sorrow
blights our hopes and plans

—and on your face the peace
of one whose whole life through,
walked with God.
Your devoted husband.

Beautiful places elicit beautiful thoughts. And after a day in that place of rapturous scenery with a loving family, my thoughts soared above issues of conflict to items of promise, hope, reconciliation, and community asseveration. It was at that moment that I rededicated myself to live out the special calling that I had announced from a pulpit at New Saint Paul twenty-six years before. I knew that my detractors would not change or go away, but I also knew that my future would not be determined by their conversion or their departure. Regardless of false friends or faithful foes, in that place of pointed salvias and conjoining geraniums, I knew what Theodore Roosevelt meant when he said, "Far better it is to dare mighty things, to win glorious triumphs, even though checkered by failure, than to take rank with those poor spirits who neither enjoy much nor suffer much, because they live in the gray twilight that knows not victory nor defeat." I knew what Leonardo da Vinci meant when he wrote, "When once you have tasted flight, you will always walk the earth with your eyes turned skyward, for there you have been and there you will always be."

I returned to Talladega renewed, revived, and recharged. I wish that I could say that we lived happily ever after, but such is not the way of this world in general nor of Talladega in particular. Before our term would conclude, the city council of Talladega would confront an issue unlike any issue the city could have anticipated, and in spite of my desire to occupy the role of peacemaker, I would find myself in the eye of a storm unlike any in the history of our city.

The city election of 1991 not only ushered in a new city council, it also returned Larry Barton to the seat of mayor. In a close election, Barton was returned to power. The fact that I was a candidate for council caused me to sit out the mayor's race. The Lawrence controversy had actually benefited Barton. He had attended meetings in support of Dr. Lawrence and had made public statements that were openly critical of the way in which the majority of the school board members had mishandled the issue. During his four-year official absence from City Hall as mayor, Barton had been accused of working actively behind the scenes to sabotage the Montgomery Administration. In one instance there was a serious entanglement between the former mayor and Talladega County Commission chairman, Steve Hurst. Commissioner Hurst publicly accused the former mayor of encouraging a woman to sue the city of Talladega. A police department jailer was convicted of raping a woman while she was an inmate at the Talladega City jail.

"According to the transcript of the trial," Hurst said, "Assistant District Attorney Julian King asked the woman who had directed her to file the claim and she testified, under oath, that former Mayor Larry Barton directed her." Hurst said he was surprised and puzzled that Barton responded to other statements he made at a county commission meeting, but had no answer to accusations that he encouraged the woman to file a lawsuit against the city. "This is just one of his behind-the-scenes tactics to try to destroy Talladega and Talladega County because he lost the mayor's race." Commissioner Hurst said Barton "offers only criticism" and he thought that none of Barton's rhetoric was meant to benefit Talladega or Talladega County. "I personally feel that he will do anything at the expense of anyone or anything for publicity or as long as people call the name Larry Barton!"

Regardless of personal suspicions, Larry Barton had been reelected. Regardless of the Vanessa Williams incident, I was committed to honor the vote of the majority and work with the mayor as an elected member of the city's governing body. When the qualifying date ended in late July, 1991, twenty-one people had tossed their hats into the ring for the five council seats. I counted myself fortunate to have been one of the five chosen and I told myself that this was an opportunity that I would not fumble.

The protests were behind and the new challenges were before me. The school board was a part of my past. The city council was a post in my future. I had run for office, reminding my constituency that not all industries relied on smokestacks.

The natural beauty of Talladega, nestled in the mountains, make her the ideal tourist attraction. The opportunity to market and partly govern this geographical wonder was one that I treasured because I had lived through enough and lived long enough to know that no opportunity was really of value unless it was recognized and claimed. I both recognized and claimed my unique privilege.

Larry Barton had won in a close election—260 votes in the runoff, 2,278 to 2,018. He had received 53 percent of the vote. Barton led heavily in Ward 1, 707 to 147, which provided him more than twice his margin of victory. The vote in Ward 1, which is predominantly black, revealed both anger and distrust of those who were incumbents. Most knew that those feelings were tied to the school board issues that had been dominant for so long. Early in the school board dispute, Barton had openly sided with Dr. Lawrence, and Dr. Lawrence's supporters didn't forget.

The incumbent mayor also tried to convince school board members to hire Dr. Lawrence, but his efforts were done behind the scenes. The local paper's editorial comment read:

"The election shows clearly that black voters here, when organized, can provide the margin of victory that won't likely be forgotten by future candidates."

As I think of Larry Barton's appeal to black voters, I am reminded of the white insurance salesmen who worked in the black community when I was a youth. We often liked them because they were civil. They smiled. They could have been rabid segregationists or Ku Klux Klan wizards. We liked them and their smiles provoked our gratitude simply because they didn't insult us with racist language.

When people who have been treated as if they were subhuman are treated like they are human, they are grateful. The day, however, is coming soon when minorities will expect more from elected officials than a church visit, a warm smile, and a returned phone call. Policy, not gesture, will become a necessity for support.

Larry Barton studied our community. He often said the right things publicly but his policies never made a positive difference. Under his administration there were no significant advances made for African-Americans in particular or for Talladegans in general. He often revealed a mean streak dropping rumors, creating divisions, and looking for "dirt" on anyone who opposed his views. He had been elected and was determined to stay elected.

I sought to be ruled by my higher self. Little did I know that my higher self would be challenged by this adversary in a way few public officials have known. But I would meet the challenge and survive. In my future clashes with this so-called "man of the people" I was destined to see the fragile fabric of a portion of our city unravel. And while I fought this force of beguiling classism, racism, and religious materialism there were many days in which it seemed that I heard Nero playing his infamous fiddle. As ancient Rome burned to the ground, Nero played on. Many people, like Nero, seemed to not know or care about what was going on.

7

A Test of My Resolve

WHILE THERE IS some truth to the saying "Be careful what you ask for, you might just get it," I have found a far more frequent reality which says, "Be careful what you resolve, it will be tested." A resolution before the test is like a building buzzing with activity. However, difficult times can somehow cause the silhouette of the same building to be lean and lonely.

The municipal law of Talladega says that the new mayor assumes duties on the first Monday in October of the year of city elections. Before Larry Barton could make our first official council meeting on October 7, 1991, a lawsuit was filed to keep him from assuming mayoral duties.

Clarence Pettus, a candidate for mayor in the Talladega general election, filed the election challenge and lawsuit seeking a writ of mandamus in circuit court on September 23rd. The lawsuit stated that the city council certified Barton's election of September 18th despite its knowledge of his failure to comply with the Alabama Fair Campaign Practices Act. The petition asked the judge to void the city council's certification of Barton as mayor because of his failure to comply with the act. That law requires candidates to file statements showing who donated money to them. The law requires candidates to file the statements from five to ten days before an election. The purpose of the law is to allow the public access to the names of the people who donate to election campaigns. Barton did complete and file the proper forms, but he had not done so during the time period specified for in the state law.

By late Monday morning, October 7th, the Clay County district judge who heard the case ruled that the city council had to revoke the certificate of election. This was the first day of our new administration. What a way to start off. Instead of dealing with simple housekeeping and departmental assignments, we walked through the door with a district judge's order telling us to revoke the mayor's certificate of election that had been given to him by the outgoing council. It was my first test.

Following the swearing-in ceremony, I asked for the floor and said, "I don't feel that we are helpless as a council. We need to know what options we have and explore them." The crowd agreed. I continued, "There is no clear-cut answer in this case."

The city attorney told us we had a few options. The council could obey the court order and revoke the certification of Barton as mayor. Council members could be held in contempt of court if the judge's order was not followed. If this was done, the previous mayor would continue to serve until a successor was elected. The council could call a new election, but unfortunately, the law didn't allow for it at this point. Or, the council could file a motion with the judge to alter, amend, or vacate the order and ask him to point out a remedy."

I decided not to act on the judge's order. Black people in an overwhelming vote had elected Larry Barton as mayor. For me to have obeyed the judge's order would have meant that I would be a part of a disenfranchisement of those voters. I did not trust Larry Barton but my constituents voted for him and I determined in my soul that I would not betray them. I knew what contempt of court could mean, but I had made a private decision and I had to live it out in my public position. As I now look back, there were, in those hours, certain signs and omens that spoke prophetically. In the month of November, 1991, one city attorney, who was defending the mayor-elect, said the Alabama League of Municipalities, in its motion, contended the order to revoke Barton's certificate of election was unconstitutional. The league claimed the court had no jurisdiction in the dispute.

The mayor-elect joked and said, "Unless I'm charged with wrongdoing, they can't do anything."

During that lighthearted moment, another city attorney suggested a remedy for the election dispute, which had not been mentioned. He said, "One remedy is criminal sanctions against the mayor."

The mayor-elect jokingly put his hands out on the table and crossed them as if waiting for the handcuffs to be put on.

We went back to the judge. He restated his order and went one step further. He ordered another election to fill the vacancy that we would create by following his mandate. On December 9th, we met as a city council, voted to hold another election, but refused to nullify the mayor-elect election as the court had ordered us. We were treading on dangerous ground, but there are some prices that you have to pay in order to have a clear conscience. Each of us who voted not to nullify the certificate of election could have been jailed and fined 200 dollars a day. We were willing to take the chance rather than disenfranchise the majority of voters who voted in our city election. In an attempt to avoid the wrath of the court, we did ask our attorney to seek a delay in the court order while we appealed his order to the Alabama State Supreme Court.

We set the special city election for mayor on Tuesday, February 10th, qualifying from December 10th to January 14th. The more I researched the matter concerning the district court's jurisdiction, the more troubling it became. For a few days, I couldn't put my finger on the problem. It was just a feeling, but a strong feeling that we were dealing with an elusive solution. Then, it hit me! Even if we had a new election, someone else could contest it because of the district court's earlier ruling. Someone could say the district court had no authority to call for a new election and we'd find ourselves confronted with a sore that wouldn't heal in spite of my best interventions.

There were three possible responses from the Supreme Court. The justices could say the order was wrong and there was a misapplication of the law. They could say Larry Barton was mayor and the failure to file was inconsequential. The court could say the judge was correct and the remedy was correct. They could affirm the district judge's decision.

Lastly, the court could affirm the judge's decision to revoke the certificate, but reject his idea of a remedy for ordering another election to fill the vacancy.

The ruling by the Supreme Court was expected to take at least six months, but the decision came less than two months later and ruled that the district court did not have authority to revoke the mayor-elect's certificate of election. The court said the basic facts were not seriously disputed. On July 16, 1991, Larry H. Barton announced his candidacy for the office of mayor of Talladega. The election was held on August 27, 1991. No candidate received a majority of votes in that election, thus a second election, or run-off, was necessary. That election was held on September 17, 1991.

On the day before the election at approximately 4 p.m., Barton filed his campaign committee disclosure form and his statement of contributions and expenditures that are required by the Fair Campaign Practices Act (FCPA). This filing was not timely. The run-off election was held on September 17th as scheduled. On the day after the election, the city council declared Barton the winner and issued him a certificate of election.

On September 23, 1991, five days after the results of the second election were declared, Clarence Pettus, a white man who had often ran unsuccessfully for mayor, filed a contest of that second election. He also asked the trial court to revoke the certificate of election issued to Barton and to order a new election. Pettus's challenge to Barton's election was based on Barton's failure to comply with the FCPA requirement that he file his campaign committee form and his Statement of Contribution and Expenditures within five days of declaring his candidacy.

The trial court, finding that Barton did not comply with the FCPA, ordered the city council to revoke Barton's certificate of election, relying on the provisions of Alabama Code 1975, 17—22A—21. The city council filed a counterclaim in which it sought a court order to establish a procedure for electing a new mayor. The trial court responded by ordering the city to hold another election. Both the city and Barton appealed the trial court's order revoking the certificate of election.

Two basic arguments were made by the city and Barton. First, although Barton did not file his statement of contributions and expenditures as required by the FCPA, he did file them prior to the election. Therefore, the trial court was without authority to order his certificate of election revoked. Second, the FCPA did not authorize a court to revoke a certificate of election issued to the winning candidate in a municipal election, because no statute granted a court such authority.

After reading the briefs of the parties and after considering the oral arguments, the court concluded that the issue presented in this case could be decided without addressing the question of whether the trial court could have revoked the certificate of election on the basis that Barton's noncompliance with the FPCA was "gross." A jurisdictional question was presented as to whether the trial court, under the provisions of 17—22A—21, had the power to revoke the certificate of election issued to Barton by the city council.

A court did not have the jurisdiction to interfere in an election result, unless a statute authorizes it to do so. Alabama Code 1975, 17—15—6, divests courts of such jurisdiction.

Municipal elections could be challenged under a few conditions:

(a) The election of any person declared elected to any office of a city or town may be contested by any person who was, at the time of the election, a qualified elector of such city or town for any of the following causes:

> 1. Misconduct, fraud, or corruption on the part of any election official, any marker, the municipal governing body or any other person.
>
> 2. The person whose election to office is contested was not eligible thereto at the time of such election.
>
> 3. Illegal votes.
>
> 4. The rejection of legal votes.
>
> 5. Offers to bribe, bribery, intimidation, or other misconduct calculated to prevent a fair, free, and full exercise of the elective franchise.
>
> (b) Any contest of such an election must be commenced within five

days after the result of the election was declared.

The Supreme Court held that under that provision, courts did not have the jurisdiction to revoke the certificate of election issued to Barton. Had Pettus filed the action before the certificate of election was issued, or if he had challenged Barton's noncompliance with the provisions of the FCPA before the election, then the court would have had jurisdiction to grant whatever relief was appropriate. The judgment of the trial court was reversed and a judgment was rendered for the appellants.

With ruling from the Supreme Court in favor of the city, we felt that we had cause to hope for a fruitful administration. The mayor was sworn in for a second time.

Clashes and Confrontations

In spite of my hopes for a peaceful term, controversy and political upheaval seemed to be drawn to us as bees are drawn to honey. Hard on the heels of the election dispute, the mayor had a major clash with the city's Civil Service Board. The clash with Civil Service began when the board objected to the mayor's hiring of two employees. The board claimed that the mayor and the city had broken the law by not opening up the position of revenue commissioner and bookkeeper so that other employees and the interested persons from the public community could apply.

Talladega, being a small town, definitely had a "good ole boy" network. You know certain folks and certain folks make things happen for you regardless of qualifications. This network had a strong opponent in Talladega in the form of the Civil Service Board. The mayor contended that he simply rehired the previous revenue commissioner in order to avoid a lawsuit. He also claimed that he didn't hire the bookkeeper, but simply transferred her from one city department to another. Civil Service wouldn't hear it. They filed a lawsuit and as a city governing body, we seemed destined to spend time, money, and energy in a world of legal briefs, courtrooms, and attorney consultations.

After months of debate and discussion, we settled the lawsuit. We removed the employee from the payroll and rehired him as a temporary worker while we advertised the position for a permanent employee. We hired the bookkeeper as a city clerk. The city clerk's position was exempt from Civil Service. We found a way to fix the lawsuit, but we had no success in containing the spirit of conflict that emanated from the halls of city government.

Councilwoman, Edythe Sims

Mrs. Sims was a thin brown-skinned woman with darting eyes. She was in her second term as a city official and she had been an active and open leader in the T. Y. Lawrence controversy. More often than seldom, Mrs. Sims would say, "I am a strong black woman," and then she would go on to make her statements or make her requests. She was as strong as she was insightful. She was courageous and hard-working. In the spirit of Sojourner Truth and Harriet Tubman, Edythe Sims would say what she meant and mean every word of what she said.

She was a retired educator who had taught her high school students strong lessons about personal commitment. She often referred to Dante's statement: "The hottest place in hell is reserved for the uncommitted." Whatever you might have said about her, no one could ever accuse Edythe Sims of being uncommitted. Heated exchanges between Mrs. Sims and Mayor Barton became commonplace. I tried to occupy the role of peacemaker, but it was not to be. In April of 1992, Mrs. Sims accused the mayor of exercising a vendetta against her and the residents of the ward that she represented. She cited her support for the previous mayor as Barton's reason for the vendetta, and claimed that the mayor had put pressure on the police department to harass residents in her ward. She called for a street meeting in her ward and invited me to listen to the concerns of her people and to speak some words of encouragement and direction, as I deemed appropriate. I consented to do so. The complaints were serious and the mood was pregnant with riot possibilities.

On the day she went to get a parade permit, the mayor and Mrs. Sims had a run-in in the corridor of City Hall.

"We got into a shouting match," she later said angrily. "He called me a fool and said I was dirt. He hollered at me, and I hollered back."

"She came in screaming, ranting, and raving like a fool," Mayor Barton said. "She told me not to touch her and I said I'm not going to touch you because I don't want to get my hands dirty."

"I also told him about that crooked and dishonest calendar that he had printed with a picture of himself and Jessie Jackson," she said. "Jessie Jackson had spoken at Talladega College's commencement. The mayor was there to welcome him. I'm just glad he didn't offer him a key to the city. The mayor had his picture taken with Reverend Jackson. He then took the picture and produced what he calls the Barton—Jackson Souvenir Calendar. He used it in the black community as if it was a public endorsement of his campaign by Jessie Jackson. The man is dishonest."

Mrs. Sims said that she believed that the mayor was involved when the city condemned some of her rental property in January. She also claimed that the mayor had harassed her and assassinated her character on local radio talk shows. She was not the only elected official who felt that way. Councilman Howard "Rip" Williams said the local radio talk shows were creating turmoil all over the city.

The radio talk shows lasted for a half hour at that time. People would call in without identifying themselves and ask questions, raise issues, and make statements. Rip Williams said, "It's the same few people. We're letting this city be dictated by a call-in talk show that has shown that it is biased. The mayor has a few friends that he programs. I'm sick of it!"

Mrs. Sims also said, "The mayor used his position to create problems for the summer food program for children, simply because I was operating it. The auditor didn't say anything in '88 when I began the program. It was never questioned until '91, when he came into office."

It was Howard Baker who asked the famous Watergate question that toppled President Nixon—"What did the president know and when did he know it?" It was Edythe Sims who first asked the question that a city, federal court, and newspapers across the nation would eventually ask.

We met at 5 P.M. on the scheduled date for the street meeting. There were about four hundred people present. They had stories of police misconduct and mayoral hostility. A lot of folks spoke that day. A middle aged light-skinned man who several people referred to as Bro Junior was the first to speak and he said, "I called City Hall and asked for some help with these wild dogs. The mayor asked me where I lived. I told him Knoxville. He said, 'Don't call me. Call Mrs. Sims. Y'all didn't vote for me.'"

A young black man in his early twenties who identified himself as Tee Tom spoke. "I was just minding my own business. I go to church. I've never been in trouble. The cops pulled me over, made me spread-eagle, and searched my car. When I asked them why, they said that the mayor had told them to crack down on Ward Two."

The media was present. Some got caught up in the media moment and became theatrical, but most were convinced that they were being singled out for persecution. As a pastor and counselor, I had learned many years prior to that day that sometimes people need to vent. They did. I listened for three hours. I took notes and informed them of the process to employ if they wanted to lodge formal complaints. The climate was explosive, but became productive. Sometimes, people just need to know that somebody is listening, that somebody cares, and that somebody respects their need to be respected. Edythe Sims stood out that day as a champion in defense of the most defenseless among her ward.

In spite of the serious nature of the charges, I withheld judgment, awaiting the outcome of a formal investigation. Although the charges were serious, they were, at that point, only charges.

Mrs. Sims was convinced that something was terribly wrong at City Hall. 26,000 dollars was reported missing from thirteen deposits that had been made during a seven-month period. The money disappeared between the office of the court clerk and the city's bank depository. Mrs. Sims began to ask for city records. Even though we turned the matter over to the Alabama Bureau of Investigation, she was not pleased. Neither was I. She called me one rainy morning.

"Dr. Patterson, we have some serious problems at City Hall."

"I agree," I said. "You are talking about the missing 26,000 dollars, aren't you?"

"I'm talking about that and some other things that I don't want to discuss over the phone. I've started my own investigation. You'll be surprised at what he is getting away with."

"What do you mean?"

"I can't tell you right now. I don't want to tip my hand. When I get access to the city records, I will let you know."

"Okay," I said, "I'll wait to hear from you on that matter when you see fit."

She added, "You know that that gag order he gave to the city employees is just an attempt to hide information. You know that, don't you?"

"As an elected official you have a right, as any other citizen, to public documents," I replied.

"I just want you to know and hear it from me. I have instructed my attorney to file a lawsuit in circuit court. I am, through my attorney, Jake Montgomery, subpoenaing all the telephone records for the city. I particularly want those of the mayor, along with all the checks and documents the mayor has paid out under his five hundred dollar spending authority. I also want to see the records of all the expenses the mayor has been reimbursed for like travel and lodging and documentation of all raises given."

"Mrs. Sims, are you telling me that the mayor has given raises to certain employees without council approval?"

"That's exactly what I'm saying. He gave them out as payment to certain people who helped him get elected. I'm telling you, he did it and is still doing it. I don't mind saying this on the telephone. I don't care who is listening. There are some illegal raises being given out at City Hall."

I responded, "I hope that you will share this information with the council president. I'm sure that Donald (Hubbard) would be very interested in researching that issue and putting a stop to it."

"I think that you are right," she said. "Mr. Hubbard is a good and honest man. I'll let you know in a few days. Thank you for listening to me. We'll talk later."

As we said goodbye, I told her to take care and that I would like to hear from her soon.

True to her word, Mrs. Sims took the matter of city records to the circuit court. The circuit judge, Jerry Fielding, ruled that the city officials had to bring telephone and invoice records for the past fifteen months to his courtroom. When the judge ruled that those records be made available for the Civil Service lawsuit, it provided Mrs. Sims with the access that she desired. The city and the Civil Service Board settled the lawsuit by agreeing that the city would pass a new ordinance. The new ordinance adopted the Civil Service system and made allowances for the two employees who were caught in the crossfire.

It was in November of 1992 that Mrs. Sims asked the question that started a process that threw our city into crisis like none it had experienced. In a regular council meeting, Mrs. Sims asked, "Who is Jerry Jackson?" The mayor answered her by saying, "Jerry is a tree stump remover. I hired him to get rid of all the tree stumps in the city." That was the only discussion aired in the public meeting at that time. Mrs. Sims said nothing more about the matter in my presence. However, she and Councilman Rip Williams began to work closely on several city projects ranging from street pavement work to grant proposals. Most of us, as council members, didn't know it, but her investigation continued.

Mrs. Sims became seriously ill and died within a few months. Even at the time of her illness, however, she was so determined to see her investigation go on that she turned over her information to Rip Williams and asked him to pursue it.

To me, the death of Mrs. Sims was another reminder of the fact that we're all in transit. It was a signal that in spite of our ingenuity, our best boast of permanence is only temporary. We are merely borrowing receptacles of which we barely comprehend. In spite of our know-how, we design nothing beyond our transit camps in our own strength. But if we are aware of what we know, then we are obligated to act on that knowledge. We must act, because it is by our acts and our actions that we create the factors that are conducive to a pleasant journey beyond the flaps on our earthly tents. We must act, because it is through our deeds that this life is a prelude and not a conclusion, and we can be certain about the place we will be settling into once we leave this transit camp. Mrs. Sims did not live to see her investigation work finished as a city councilwoman, but she sent forth the message to us all that Bernadette Garzarelli was right when she wrote "turning down the wrong road is a part of the journey, and finding the way back is a challenge that we can all live up to."

Maintaining a Good Memory

If you've ever forgotten an appointment, birthday, or an anniversary, you can verify the importance of memory in our lives. Memory is a kind of umbilical cord which keeps us tied to the wisdom of the past and prevents grace-defeating arrogance, self-righteousness, and the tendency to pass judgment on others. Memory has a way of pulling us down from our self-erected pedestals as it instructs us in who we are. Memory challenges—if not laughs at—our self-righteousness and condemns our judgmental attitudes. Recalling truth, we are forced to confess our capacity for sinfulness and admit our disposition toward evil. In the face of another person's difficulties, we quietly confess, "There but for the grace of God go I." When memory fails, God's wonderful grace toward us is thwarted, and our grace toward others is aborted. However, when memory works, we act as the vessels and vehicles of God's grace.

As the days went by, there were rumors in City Hall that ranged from the remarkable to the ridiculous. Some of the rumors carried with them very serious charges. The issue of illegal raise was one that seemed to have a life of its own. However, the mayor denied any wrongdoing and assured the council that everything was in order regarding pay scales for all city employees. I was willing to give him the benefit of the doubt, and my trust, until such time as I felt that it had been betrayed. I had made a personal vow to support the mayoral office and honor the wishes of the voting majority in our city.

It wasn't easy. In place after place, people would ask, "What's going on at City Hall? I hear that we have a mess going on!"

I would listen and reply, "I have not seen anything official to indicate anything wrong beyond the rumors. Only time will tell." This was not simply a coined answer for inquiring minds, it was my belief system. I lived by it. I lived with it. I remembered my resolution. The pressure was mounting. Hostility was rising. Trouble was brewing. I could see it on the faces of some of my fellow council members. Their eyes glinted with a strange mixture of pleasure and pain.

It started in February of 1993. Several African-Americans, who had strong ties to the mayor, began to call me. They expressed concerns that the mayor was about to be "set up" because "we" helped put him back in office. At first, I felt that the calls were simply born out of fear. However, as time moved on, they seemed rehearsed and by April of 1993, I was convinced that the callers were being programmed to ascertain my mood. I gave them my usual answer, which did not convey the idea that I had made up my mind one way or the other. The Persian proverb, "He who wants a rose must respect the thorn" was uppermost in my mind. Some of the very people who called were some that not only had strong ties to the mayor, but also had actively worked to keep me out of the council seat I was occupying at the time.

Somehow, despite the extremities of the conditions, whether the scorching, manipulative hatred from my enemies or the chilling prospects of my public isolation in taking on the candidate that received 75 percent of the vote from my ward, I was determined to be faithful to my calling and fruitful in my service. There is an admonition in the Bible which says, "Recall the former days." I did and as I recalled them, I once again remembered what the white miner had told me many years before. I remembered how he warned me about those blacks in our own community that could be used to contain us because they lived among us. I never made the callers aware of my suspicion. I simply listened, gave my standard reply, and waited for events to unfold.

8

City Hall in Crisis

I T WAS AN EARLY May morning. The phone rang. It was Rip Williams. "Dr. Patterson, this is Rip. I know it's early, but you are the police liaison from the council and I need to talk with you today! What would be a good time?"

"How about lunch?"

Rip is the kind of guy that you feel like you've known all your life. He owned a very successful heating and cooling business. He's about six foot three inches, 230 pounds, and has a heavy mustache and a grin that is both mischievous and warm. He is soft-spoken most of the time, and laid back in demeanor. However, I could sense some stress in his voice that morning.

I arrived at the restaurant, the Dinner Bell, around 11:20 a.m. They have a chicken-fried steak that is only matched by their famous fried green tomatoes. The Dinner Bell is a small, down-home Talladega restaurant that specializes in southern cooking and hospitality with desserts that are homemade, like peach and apple cobblers. It's the crust that makes their cobblers so great. It's flaky, crisp, and usually sprinkled with a tad of cinnamon basted with butter. You can smell it as you approach from the sidewalk.

Rip showed up about five minutes after I arrived. He had a briefcase and wanted to sit in a booth near the back. "Horace, the first thing I want to say is that I didn't start out to set up the mayor. I know what folks are saying. Larry is the one who started the rumors about me wanting to be mayor. I might run for mayor at the next election, but what I want to talk with you about now has nothing to do with my political aspirations."

I said, "Okay, Rip, let's see what you've got."

"All right. You know that Mrs. Sims turned over her information to me after she became ill. She asked me to pursue the investigation because this Jerry Jackson person that the mayor claims has been cutting and grinding tree stumps doesn't really exist. When we checked the Social Security number for him, we found out that the number and address belonged to my cousin, Jerry Wilson. Now Jerry Wilson is a tree surgeon, but he swears that he has not been working for the city in a contract with Larry Barton at the rate of the checks that have been made to Jerry Jackson. When an income tax withholding form for this mysterious Jerry Jackson was returned to City Hall by the postal service, the workers asked Larry for a new Social Security number and address. Larry gave them the Social Security number of a dead person and the address of a woman who said she had never heard of Jerry Jackson and he definitely has not lived in her house."

I shook my head. Rip continued.

"It gets even better. Nobody has ever seen Jerry Jackson. We have paid out more than 18,000 dollars to this person for grinding stumps and nobody has ever seen him but the mayor."

"Wait a minute, Rip. How could we have paid a nonexistent worker? Don't we pay by check? Who picked up the checks?"

"The mayor did. He is the only person who has ever picked up or cashed these Jerry Jackson checks."

I put my head in my hand, closed my eyes, and asked the obvious question. "Are all of the checks less than 500 dollars?"

"You got it ! Every check requested by the mayor for Jerry Jackson was under 500 dollars. As you know, that comes under his spending authority. He didn't need approval from us, nor did he need council support because he kept the check amounts under his spending authority."

"Rip, this is very serious!"

"I know. That's why I wanted to meet with you as police liaison. I am going to file a police incident and offense report alleging possible fraud. I have already spoken with the police. They know that my cousin's name and address were used on this Jerry Jackson's paperwork at City Hall."

"Rip," I said, "I will support the police investigation. This is far too serious a matter to ignore. When you file your report, ask the investigating officers to contact me."

"I will."

Investigating the Mayor

Detective Ken Sisk and Captain W.E. "Pee-Wee" Hurst were assigned the case to either prove or disprove the existence of the mysterious stump grinder, Jerry Jackson. I met with them and simply said, "Gentlemen, do your job. This is not a political hot potato. This is a matter for law enforcement. I will support you as liaison. Do your jobs and let the chips fall where they may."

We were in for ten stressful months. Both officers knew what was at stake and how it could affect them and their families. They knew that their days would be long and eventually both of them would be attacked. Their family members would suffer the emotional toll of investigating a popular political figure in a small town. Yet, in spite of this, the two officers revealed a tenacious mindset to see the matter to a conclusion.

"The only thing I ask is that we are allowed to do our jobs," Ken Sisk said. "I've seen how vicious this mayor can be. I don't need anybody to hold my hand, but I do want to be able to follow leads, gather evidence, and refer it to the proper authorities without having roadblocks thrown in my face at every turn. You know what I mean?"

"Ken, I understand you," I said, "You have my word."

"This is a criminal investigation," Captain Hurst said. "At some point, I am certain that we will turn over information to the F.B.I. The Feds will not be intimidated by anyone. I just want to make sure that we have enough room and time to make our case. I will tell you now that I am 90 percent convinced that federal laws have been broken. The only sighting of Jerry Jackson was by one of our U.F.O. spotters who said he saw him having lunch at the Dinner Bell with Elvis."

I smiled and remarked, "I wonder if they ordered the country-fried steak and fried green tomatoes?"

"No sir! According to that source, they were both vegetarians. And Jerry Jackson is not his real name. His real name is Bubba Gonzales, or something."

We all laughed. The mayor had described Jerry Jackson as being around six feet tall, a minority—possibly a mix of Hispanic and African-American, with a very muscular build.

On May 24, 1993, I received some audio tapes in the mail. The tapes were mailed in a letter-sized envelope with one tape in a smaller envelope inside. The addresses were printed in large letters, like a child's printing. As I listened to the tape, I was completely convinced that it had been doctored. There was a female voice and the discussions indicated that the white female was Mrs. Sue Horn, our personnel director. The tapes suggested that the mayor was being set up by his political enemies.

"I think they got him this time," said the female.

The male voice replied, "Don't be too sure. Larry is a good man. He wouldn't do anything wrong."

The female voice responded, "I'm not saying he did anything wrong. I don't know all of what he did, but I do think that we've got him this time. I have been gathering information here in the personnel office and we are going to nail him one way or another."

By that time, council members knew that the city had written checks totaling more than 18,000 dollars to Jerry Jackson in 1992. When the questions came up concerning the identity of Jackson, the mayor took the responsibility for purchase orders and invoices from Mrs. Horn and gave it to a bookkeeper.

The day following my reception of the tapes, we called a special council meeting at the request of Councilman James Spratlin. Jim began the discussion by addressing Police Chief Mike Hamlin and Personnel Director Sue Horn. "Over the weekend, a number of constituents had questions for me that I wasn't able to officially answer. Is there an inquiry or investigation regarding tree-cutting service?"

Hamlin responded, "Yes, sir, there is."

Jim went on to question Mrs. Horn if she had been able to function and do her job in her office. She responded, "Yes, sir. No problem."

We had heard that the mayor had changed the lock on Mrs. Horn's office door, citing a need for security amid Mrs. Horn's "sudden, unannounced departure." She had taken off on Thursday at noon and didn't work on Friday. I asked her if she had been taking comp time. She answered that she had and said that she had notified the mayor's secretary of her decision to take comp time. The issue in most of our minds was whether a lock change on the door to the personnel office was an attempt to block or slow down the criminal investigation that had begun.

We passed a motion requiring that every bill paid have a purchase order and every payment for contract labor be accompanied by a contract. We hoped that this would prevent further opportunities for abuse of a system that was vulnerable to misuse.

As we moved along in that meeting, we discovered that the issue of the lock change was not peculiar just to us. Chief Hamlin confirmed that he met with FBI officials during the day and said that F.B.I. investigators would be coming to Talladega. The chief told us that the key for the new lock on the personnel office wouldn't work to lock the door at the end of the day. The chief and Mrs. Horn had struggled with the two keys until one broke. They called the locksmith for repair work. The troubling matter about the lock change was that the mayor was quoted in the newspaper on the day before our meeting as saying the locks on the personnel office door were changed at the request of District Attorney Robert Rumsey. The mayor had said that the office was sealed at the request of the D.A. and the chief of police, but the seal consisted of pieces of red tape placed from the door to the jamb and over the keyhole on the doorknob, so it would be detectable if someone entered the office on the weekend.

Only the lock from the hallway into Mrs. Horn's office was changed. The lock on a door from the mayor's secretary's office was unchanged. That doorknob locked from the side of the mayor's secretary's office. This meant that entry through the mayor's secretary's office could and would be undetected.

Mrs. Horn told us that she was made aware of the press release on the Friday afternoon that the lock was changed. She said, "In a conversation with the D. A.'s office, I asked if they were aware of this. They told me they were not aware of my locks being changed or my office being secured. I was told by investigators that they went immediately to the mayor's office and asked for the keys to the new lock. I was called by the investigators shortly afterwards and asked to come to my office and verify that nothing had been tampered with, removed, or added. At that time, the district attorney's office told the chief of police, in my presence, that they were not concerned with any personnel records in my office. That they just wanted to be sure that nothing had been tampered with since the change of locks. They instructed the chief to turn the keys back over to me. Everyone at City Hall has known for years that there's not but one key to the personnel office, and it's in my possession."

More Tapes

In a matter of days, I received another set of tapes. I had turned the first set over to the chief of police. This time I refused to play the new set and hand-carried them to the chief's office. I had a feeling that I wouldn't have to play them to know what was on them. I was right. This time the mayor said that he received a tape as well. When I turned over the first tapes, I simply made a generic statement, saying, "They might shed some light on the motives of the Jackson case." I knew that my statement would elicit more tapes because the sender wanted public discussion and debate. Other councilmen followed my lead. When they received tapes, they refused to go into detail and simply turned them over to the chief of police.

The last set of tapes was placed in our mail at City Hall. This time, Mayor Barton hurriedly called a press conference and claimed that he had also received a set. He played his copy of the tapes for City Hall employees and the media. Once again, the female voice appeared to be the voice of Personnel Director Sue Horn, possibly in a telephone conversation discussing personalities inside and outside City Hall with references to the Jerry Jackson matter. Once again, there were long pauses between some of her comments on the tape, and this time, no other voice could be heard.

Mrs. Horn said she had never given permission for any of her conversations to be taped. She said, "If, in fact, anyone has a tape of my voice on the telephone, then my home was violated and it was obtained illegally." She said investigators were aware of the tapes. "In my opinion, they're much more interested in how those tapes might have been obtained than who's saying what about whom."

District Attorney Robert Rumsey, a tall, muscular, white man who had played football at the University of Alabama for the legendary Paul "Bear" Bryant, addressed the "tape issue" in a press conference. He said, "A complaint was made last Wednesday morning to my office by two private citizens alleging that private conversations that they had at their homes were illegally eavesdropped upon and illegally recorded. That would be a crime under Alabama law and federal law. Pursuant to that complaint, that is being investigated as any complaint of criminal conduct would be, a tape was turned over by another private citizen that allegedly contains private telephone conversations of at least one of the citizens who made the complaint. I feel compelled to say that these tapes have no bearing on the Jerry Jackson investigation."

The D.A.'s public comment cancelled out the usefulness of the tapes. The focus of the investigation had not been deflected and the act of illegally taping Mrs. Horn did not ring prophetic bells fulfilling the hopes that the investigation would just go away.

One of the members of our parish, Mr. Eddie Stowers, a man of clear insight, once said to me, "Most folk try to find their own inn before nightfall." I remembered his wisdom and watched with keen interest the events that would send people to the places where they would feel most safe.

9

Who Is Jerry Jackson? The Mayor's Explanation

On May 19, 1993, with a straight face, the mayor claimed that Jerry Jackson was a Hispanic transient tree-trimmer and stump remover who worked for the city at $100 per day. At that rate, Jackson would have spent at least 180 days in Talladega digging up stumps in 1992. The mayor claimed that several storms and tornadoes had blown down hundred of trees during the past few years. Rescue workers and street department personnel used chainsaws to cut the broken trees as low as possible. He was correct about the storms and tornadoes blowing down trees. He was right about the work of rescue workers and city personnel. However, it seemed to stretch things a bit when he claimed that there were more than 2,000 stumps in the city. And it was really a stretch to imagine that this man could have worked for 180 days in a city with a population of 19,000 people and no one reputable, other than the mayor, saw him at City Hall.

Jamie Grace

Jamie Grace was an attractive African-American woman in her mid-thirties who was chief of the Talladega County United Narcotic Office. The mayor claimed that he hired Jerry Jackson at Jamie's request. According to the mayor, Jackson was doing undercover work for Jamie while he was grinding up stumps.

The story could not be validated or challenged because Jamie was found dead on Monday, August 3rd, 1992. Her death was ruled a suicide. It was tragic that this young life budding with so much promise had been cut short. It was even more tragic that Jamie's name would later be attached to this sad story of the mysterious stumpgrinder.

I knew Jamie Grace. A member of my parish had done undercover work with her. He had infiltrated a drug ring and helped in the prosecution as a witness. The district attorney knew about it, I knew, and several other people very close to me knew. The strange thing about the mayor's story concerning Jerry Jackson, Jamie Grace, and himself was that nobody knew what was going on but the three of them. And of the three, the mayor was the only one available for comment. The media had a field day. According to the mayor, Jackson had left town and gave no forwarding address.

Missing Checks at City Hall

As the investigation went forth, several incidents seemed orchestrated to stop it. Ken Sisk, the hard-nosed detective who sported a heavy mustache with thick light-brown hair, discovered that several of the checks made out to and cashed by the mysterious stumpgrinder were missing. The missing checks were drawn on the city's general fund accounts, and were written in September, October, and November of 1991, and January, February, June, and July of 1992.

The mayor said he believed that the police had lost the checks. He said, "If there's anything missing, they've lost it in their Keystone Kops atmosphere." The council simply passed a motion asking the two banks involved for their help in replacing the missing checks.

Barton Cashed Checks for Jerry Jackson

The municipal court clerk, Willis Whatley, said the mayor had cashed several checks written to Jerry Jackson in the court office. The checks were always between 250 and 400 dollars. The mayor had cashed a Jerry Jackson check in the court office as late as May 3, 1993. Mr. Whatley said, "The checks would already be endorsed by the subject when he (Barton) would bring them in. Both secretaries in my office and myself have fresh knowledge of Barton cashing the checks. Jackson's signature was almost illegible. If I didn't know what it was supposed to be, I would not have been able to read it." He said Barton cashed two checks written to Jackson on February 26, 1993. "From time to time, he would come in and couldn't get to the bank, so we would cash them for him."

Barton said Jackson was "alive and well" when he left Talladega a few weeks before Rip Williams filed his police report. He said Jackson did business as Jerry's Tree Service, based somewhere in Georgia. Jackson, however, did not have a business license to operate in Talladega, according to the revenue commissioner. The commissioner said there was a business license for Jerry's Tree Service at 205 Grizzle Lane, the same address that was listed on the tax form at City Hall for Jerry Jackson. But that Jerry's Tree Service was owned by Jerry Wilson, the cousin of Rip Williams. When contacted, Wilson said that he had never heard of a Jerry Jackson doing stump-grinding or tree work in Talladega.

Barton countered by saying that he asked the revenue commissioner if Jerry's Tree Service had a city license. He said, "When I talked to the revenue commissioner, whenever it was—several months ago—I just asked if Jerry's Tree Service had a license and he said, 'Yes, he does.' I had no reason to pursue it any further." He said it didn't occur to him that there were two businesses called Jerry's Tree Service. "That never even crossed my mind."

The mayor said that Jackson left Talladega, headed to work in Atlanta and Mississippi. When asked if he were making any efforts to bring Jackson back to Talladega, Barton replied, "If I knew where to start I'd make an effort. The last I heard he was in Atlanta."

Barton Bought and Sold Property for Jerry Jackson

William Cooper had become an angry man. Mr. Cooper, a white man, had bought a house located at 912 Hobson Avenue. He spent his spare moments renovating it and had sunk 15,000 dollars into the project. The problem that gave Mr. Cooper fits was that he bought the property from the ever-elusive Talladega celebrity, Jerry Jackson. Mr. Cooper, however, never met Jackson in person. When the name Jerry

Jackson appeared in the newspaper and was discussed on radio programs, Mr. Cooper thought that name sounded familiar. It turned out that it was the name on the deed of the property that he had bought. The person that Mr. Cooper had dealt with and paid his money to for the property was Mayor Larry Barton. By the time this matter hit the ears of the community, the mayor was claiming that Jackson had removed 400 to 500 tree stumps all over town.

Mr. Cooper had put new siding and flooring into the Hobson Avenue house. Mayor Barton said, "It was a piece of property the city had condemned. We were fixing to condemn it. We had looked at paying the back taxes on it and cleaning it up or burning it down." The mayor said the city decided not to buy the house, but Jerry Jackson chose to buy it. "I just wanted the house fixed up or destroyed," Barton said. "Mr. Cooper doesn't have anything to worry about. The state gave Jerry the deed, and Jackson transferred the deed to Cooper." The mayor said Jackson brought the deed to him. "I'm a little fuzzy on when it was notarized and signed." The mayor had gotten the deed notarized by a notary who knew him and trusted him and therefore notarized the document at his request.

Barton said Jackson was supposed to meet Cooper at the mayor's office to make the real estate transaction, and "Cooper was late or something." Barton said that Jackson left the deed with him for Cooper to pick up, and Cooper gave Barton cash in an envelope when he picked up the deed.

Barton said he didn't know how much money was in the envelope, which he said might have been sealed. The house was sold to the state for back taxes on May 10, 1988, and state records showed the city of Talladega and Barton inquired about buying the property in early November of 1992. Barton wrote a letter to the state and said that the city was no longer interested in the property. In the letter, Barton said another person, Jerry Jackson, wanted to buy the property. He then included in that letter a cashier's check from Jerry Jackson to the Revenue Department for $669.42. This was the amount of taxes owed.

At the time when this information became public, the amount of profit made on the real estate deal was not clear, but in a matter of months, Bill Barnett, a federal prosecuting attorney, would say that Barton took the money from checks written to Jackson. "Since there are no groceries to be bought and no bills to be paid, this was mad money for Mayor Barton. With that mad money, the mayor called off a real estate deal that the city was in and bought the house for 699 dollars in back taxes. He then sold the house for 6,900 dollars. It came back to him in cash and it's laundered," Barnett said.

All that we knew at that time was that Mr. Cooper had angrily said that he had paid a lot more for the property than 699 dollars. Mr. Cooper declined at that time to tell us how much he had paid for the property. Barton said he did not remember how much money Cooper gave him.

Jackson took legal possession of the property on December 18, 1992. On the afternoon of January 25, 1993 in the county courthouse, Barton filed the deeds passing the property from the previous owners to the state and from the state to Jackson.

Meanwhile, Jackson decided that "he was so busy that he'd rather get rid of it," said Barton. "So I handled it for him. That's why I know there's a Jerry Jackson."

Surging Tensions

City Hall was fast becoming the talk of the town and the talk of the state. The Jerry Jackson fallout story was increasingly ranking as one of the best known stories, though arguably it was one of the least understood and consequently, the worst discussed. My conversations with the mayor grew less and less frequent, as we seemed destined to clash over the role of the police department in the Jackson investigation. Whenever we discussed the matter, I urged him to back off, give them a chance to do their jobs, and if he was innocent, time would exonerate him. The council made a point not to accuse him publicly or share our own personal suspicions in a public forum. We operated with the "innocent-until-proven-guilty" public face, even though we each had private doubts and burgeoning apprehensions. The whole mess was bad for our city's image and neither councilman that I spoke with approached the matter gleefully.

Prior to our June 7th council meeting, Council President Donald Hubbard, a Desert Storm veteran, called me at home. Donald had heard that the mayor was going to go on the attack and said, "I want you to know that I'm not going to put up with a lot of foolishness today. This Jackson thing is creating divisions among city workers, friends, and even family members."

I said, "You're right. There is a lot of fallout, but I think that we should stay on course. We know a bit more than folks who are removed from this issue. We are going to have to handle matters as quietly as possible."

"I don't think that's going to be possible," he said with a sigh in his voice and a drop in tone.

I responded, "I've asked the mayor to back off the police department. I hope that he will listen for his own good and the good of the city."

"Well, I hope he'll listen to you because he's sure not listening to me."

The mayor came to the meeting with a prepared memorandum in which he gave up his spending authority, and told his side of the Jerry Jackson story, which starred him as a victim of vindictive people who wanted him out. He assured the citizens of Talladega that Jerry Jackson did exist and had been paid for his services. He went on to exonerate himself of any illegal act and commented on how sad it was that hate disrupted the community for the sake of the selfish wants of a few.

It was vintage Barton. He rallied his troops. Larry Barton had always claimed to be the common man's man. His supporters called the talk shows and called the council members. It was the same old song:

"I'm calling for the mayor. Y'all need to leave him alone. He's a good man. He wants to help the city. It's them big shots that hate him. No matter, though, people been trying to get Larry all his days. He's smart. He'll have an ace up his sleeve and in the end the people who fight him will have egg on their face."

The Barton supporters in City Hall were mobilized. Some attacked Captain Hurst and Detective Sisk. "I'm not going to tell them anything" was the sentiment of several city employees. Each day, the climate grew thicker. What started out as noncooperative spirit escalated into open hostility. Some employees began to speak the language of the legal area, saying, "I'm not going to tell them anything unless my lawyer is present."

I heard from several groups. The Barton supporters appealed to me to use my influence to curb or stop the investigation. The Barton antagonists sought to find out where I stood. The Barton watchers started watching me to measure my brand of leadership.

My church members simply said, "We love you. We're glad you are where you are because we know that you will do the right thing and the right thing is always the best thing."

The Barton memorandum elicited a strong editorial response from our local newspaper titled: "Barton is responsible for Jackson Controversy." The newspaper defended itself against Barton's allegations of yellow journalism, and stated that Barton's self-serving statement at the council meeting Monday was erroneous, filled with innuendoes, and designed to divert the public's attention from the questions surrounding Jerry Jackson.

The newspaper left it to its readers to decide if the paper had been engaged in innuendoes, rumors, or yellow journalism. The editorial went on to say that the paper had been critical of Barton in the past because of his blatant political motivation in attacking members of the Talladega City Council, his ongoing feud with local attorney Jake Montgomery, and his attempts to plant stories detrimental to political opponents. If he behaved in the future as he had in the past, the article said, the newspaper would continue to be critical of him.

All he had to do, according to the paper, was introduce Jerry Jackson to the citizens of Talladega.

Ed Fowler, the editor of the *Daily Home,* was steaming when he wrote that editorial. Ed was committed to holding politicians' feet to the fire. Ed is a native-born Southerner whose love for the New South was probably born at a time when the Old South was an embarrassment. I had tried to help Larry Barton develop a relationship with Ed Fowler, but my efforts were to no avail. Ed simply wanted the city to go forward. He had invested a lot of time, money, and energy to that end. He was like a fresh breeze blowing because he saw the potential of our city while at the same time demonstrating the strength to deal with threats to our future.

Without trying or even being aware of it, Providence was shaping me and moving me from the position of being a black leader to simply becoming a leader in our community. I don't know exactly how it happened, but it did. It seemed as if the deepening stressors of the crisis in city hall ushered me and pressed me into this place of responsibility and privilege. I had always believed that reputation is what people think you are, but character is what you really are. A crisis doesn't make character, but it certainly reveals character. It seemed as if this crisis was somehow driving me toward a place of leadership that I could not avoid. My enemies were still active, both black and white, but the weapons that they forged against me did not prosper.

One day as I raced across a windswept parking lot as drops of rain seemed to tear at my clothing, I happened upon two of my enemies. One was a middle-aged blond-haired white female. She had worked against my election to the city council. She and her black housekeeper had passed out literature in my ward for my opponents, even though she did not live in my ward. She had, with the spirit of a "Willie Lynch," told black voters that she knew what was best for them.

The other was a portly black female who had been a Judas during the Lawrence controversy with the school board. She had attended our community meetings for the purpose of getting information so that she could inform the opposition of our plans.

They were engaged in rapid and intense dialogue. When they looked around and saw me, one sheepishly spoke, not really certain of what I had heard. On most days, one of them could fake a grin, but not on that windy and rainy day. Here we were in a crisis like no other we'd seen, and these two were still caught up in the bondage of pettiness. Sometimes a duck doesn't have to walk like a duck for you to know that it's a duck. Sometimes, a quack is enough to make the diagnosis.

While I did not know exactly where we were headed as a city, my determination intensified to see things as they were and not permit the little things to get in my way.

In mid-August, we were hit with another strange revelation of contract workers. There were five: James Jelks, J. C. Dark, Rufus Dark, Rufus Bragg, and Joe Dark. Nobody knew who they were, yet each one had been paid by the city as contract workers. None of them were listed in the telephone book. We had no address for any of them, but records showed that they'd all been paid between $350 and $430 a piece.

When confronted with the names and issues, the mayor said, "These are individuals who have done street work cleaning up lots, and cleaning out the old depot." He said he believed that J. C. Dark and Joe Dark were the same person, but he couldn't remember exactly what each person did or when. "They're all legitimate people—someone's son or grandson. I didn't realize it was important to get a history of their mom and dad just to perform a service for the city. As far as telling you where they live, I wasn't worried about addresses," said the mayor. "The city wouldn't have tax withholding forms on the five, since each was paid less than 600 dollars during the year, because the city isn't required to file tax withholding on contract workers who earn less than that amount. It looks funny, the way I handled the Jerry Jackson thing. He did what he was hired to do and more.

"At some point in the future," Barton continued, "I may have to come forward with information about Jackson that is very sensitive. I've received letters from Jerry postmarked in Mississippi and Ohio. In his last letter, he said he was going into the hospital. Jerry Jackson does exist. Anybody we've paid a check to, that I'm aware of, does exist. There has been nothing bogus at the mayor's office. If I had been going to do anything illegal or wrong, I never would have left records. They never would have found cancelled checks or memos where I authorized payment. I'd have destroyed the records. I didn't get off the boat yesterday. It's an attempt to embarrass this administration and myself, but I will serve out my term."

On September 9, the mayor sent a memo to Police Chief Mike Hamlin, demanding all documents that had been removed from city hall as part of the Jackson investigation be returned. He also requested a list of all expenses generated by the investigation. In the course of their work, Detective Sisk and Captain Hurst seized several records from the bookkeeper at City Hall. The bookkeeper requested the return of the records, but the investigating officers refused the request. The mayor's letter read:

> I am disappointed that one or more detectives go on a witch hunt and go through city documents and take whatever they want without approval and then refuse to give copies of said documents.

In that same memo, the mayor also instructed the police chief to provide an itemized listing of telephone expenses, man-hours, and trips involved in the Jerry Jackson investigation and "to come up with a total dollar amount spent."

The chief sent a memo to the bookkeeper asking what documents had been requested and not received, and what investigator refused to turn the documents over. The chief's public statement was, "This is a criminal investigation, and I am not at liberty nor do I intend to make any public comment on any aspect of this investigation. I am in the process of developing a response to the mayor's memo. I will comply the best I can without jeopardizing a criminal investigation."

Council members read the mayor's memo as an obvious attempt to impede the Jerry Jackson investigation. Up to that point, while the relationship had been strained, it was at least civil. The letter to the chief set off a chain reaction, which evolved into open hostility in spite of my best efforts to curb it. For a few weeks, there was a feeling that we just might get through this mess without a mayor-council showdown. We were mistaken. It was like sitting in the dentist's chair and thinking that the pain injection had gone to work: just when we were about to get into the piped music the drill suddenly hit a live nerve.

I had given the police department my word that I would support them in their investigative work. The time had come for behavioral intervention and legislative support. It was time for my walk to measure up to my talk. It was time to take away the mayor's appointing authority.

Nobody had to be a rocket scientist to see that. Council President Donald Hubbard had a new ordinance drawn up. The mayor was out of town on vacation. We passed a new ordinance that rescinded an ordinance that we had approved earlier. Ordinance 1301 gave the mayor appointing authority under the city's Civil Service system, clearing up questions about who had the authority to hire, fire, and discipline employees. It gave the mayor supervision and control of "all other officers in the city." It also included supervision of department heads.

The ordinance we adopted defined each city department and its head, and gave appointing authority over each department to the appropriate department head. In the city council, we named ourselves as the appointing authority over all department heads and over all employees for whom a department head was not provided for in the ordinance.

After the meeting, Donald Hubbard said, "Well, gentlemen, we'd better get ready. When Larry gets back in town, he will go haywire."

Rip Williams said, "I know this much. We have done the right thing here. If we had sat back and let him bully the police department, we would have been less than men. It's just time to circle the wagons and wait for the attack."

I responded, "We had no choice. I hate it, but we have drawn our line in the sand. No matter what this is today, I am convinced that I know what it isn't. It isn't a mistake. Let's just be prayerful and hope that this investigation will be over soon."

We all knew that it was just a matter of time before each of us would be dealt as much misery as the mayor and his supporters could deal out.

After I left City Hall, I felt the need to pray quietly at the altar. It was a Thursday evening. No one was in the church but the Lord, myself, the massive ceilings above my head, the soft carpet beneath my knees, the Holy Communion table before my eyes, and the crisis that I was now certain would not go away. There is something unfathomably therapeutic about prayer when you hit the needy places in your life. This was such a time. I prayed that we would be equal to the tasks ahead. I prayed the prayer that is so often prevalent in African-American churches—"Lord, don't move my mountain, but give me strength to climb. Lord, don't take away my stumbling block, but lead me all around."

After prayer time, I was ready to forge ahead. We had decided against making any public statements explaining our actions. To have done so would have made a bad matter worse at the time. The time would come for public statements.

Ralph Waldo Emerson once said:

> My life is for itself and not for a spectacle... What I must do is all that concerns me, not what the people think. There is a time in every man's education when he arrives at the conviction that envy is ignorance; that imitation is suicide; that he must take himself for better or worse as his portion; that though the wide universe is full of good, no kernel of nourishing corn can come to him, but through his toil bestowed on that plot of ground which is given to him to till. The power which resides in him is new in nature, and none but he knows what that is which he can do, nor does he know until he has tried... Trust thyself; every heart vibrates to that iron string. Accept the place that divine providence has found for you, the society of your contemporaries, the connection of events. Great men have always done so...

When the mayor returned to the city, he launched attack after attack at the city council. His exact words were that we were "cowardly, underhanded, and spineless" for the action we had taken removing his appointing authority. He said he had heard remarks all over town about our action, and said he was using other people's words in calling us cowardly, spineless, and underhanded.

At our next council meeting, the mayor lashed out as he addressed the council, saying, "While I was out of town, you caught me with my back turned and you done me dirty. You've tried to lie me out of office, but I'm going to be here."

Donald Hubbard leaned over to his mike, flush-faced with his eyes fixed on the mayor, and said, "Okay! This is it! We're not going to take this any longer. Mr. Mayor, you can call a press conference if you want to, but at this time, I am asking you to remove yourself from the council table."

The mayor stood up and stormed out of the council chambers only to return later to a seat at the back of the chamber. We continued to deal with city business such as paying invoices, approving travel, and adopting resolutions and ordinances. We stayed on our course.

The mayor did have his own press conference, where he said, "They are trying to make me look like a criminal. I've wondered if it was a smoke screen. I haven't done anything illegal. You've got two council members who want to be mayor. When they take me out of office, there will be footprints in this concrete where they dragged me out. I think I'm like a war veteran; when we've got peace, I'm miserable. The council is operating like a bunch of cowards. I will veto the ordinance."

The mayor vetoed the ordinance to no avail. The veto was overridden.

Enter Jake Montgomery

Jake Montgomery, a silver-haired middle-aged man of average build with discerning eyes, is the kind of lawyer that you want in a foxhole. He is brilliant and bold. His passion is easily discernible. He didn't trust Larry Barton. Barton hated him and saw his ghost in every move the council had made.

Jake is an immaculate dresser. There is a rumor in Talladega that Jake's body rejects any suit that is not tailor-made. *Gentlemen's Quarterly* does not set the standard for Jake's dress attire, but it's possible that it could be the other way around. I guess I've never known Jake when he didn't drive a Jaguar, puff on his smoking pipes, and practice law with the zeal of one who's answered a calling—like me becoming a minister.

Jake's ties to city government were deep and solid. He was the older brother of the previous mayor, George Montgomery, and he had been a city attorney for many years. Larry Barton had ironically hired him during his first administration. Jake had never lost a case in court for the city. In fact, he was the attorney who had represented Edythe Sims in the Civil Service issue, where the city settled the case short of a trial. Jake knew the Civil Service rules and regulations because he had participated in their development. As we moved ahead, we knew that we would need strong legal assistance not only for our battle with the mayor, but also because we were sensing some serious employee problems.

Ethics Charges Against Rip Williams

Mayor Barton filed ethics charges against Rip Williams in late October, 1993. We had put out some of the fires by issuing a written public statement wherein we explained our council actions on removing the mayor as the appointing authority for city employees and by passing an ordinance regarding tape recordings of conversations. Mayor Barton often boasted that he had tapes on everybody and he used those tapes and would use them whenever he needed. The law in the state of Alabama states that a person does not violate the law if he is a party to the conversation and chooses to record it. However, that state law did not prohibit a city from regulating the use of its property or the behavior of its employees and elected officials while performing their duties.

We passed an ordinance that made it illegal to record citizens with city property without explaining to the party that he or she was being taped. The mayor was furious. He had made so public his habit of taping calls that we knew that he would not approve the ordinance. We explained that tape recordings are intimidating to the average person. We shared our belief that no representative of the city should attempt to intimidate anyone by taping conversations and especially should not threaten to use secretly recorded conversation at a later date for intimidation purposes. The ordinance did not stop any employee from recording. It simply required that common courtesy be given to those being recorded, that they be informed.

The public statement was well received. The mayor went after Rip. Ethics Commission Investigator James D. Foster wrote to Rip: "On behalf of the members of the Alabama Ethics Commission, I regret to inform you that the commission has received a request from Mayor Larry Barton to conduct an investigation into alleged violations of law committed by you which may come under the purview of the Alabama Ethics Law." Mayor Barton asked the commission to investigate Rip's company, Howard Williams, Inc., which Barton said billed and was paid for work performed on city property. Barton also contended that Rip, acting as a city councilman, voted to pay himself for that work.

The Alabama Ethics Commission cleared Rip of any wrongdoing in connection with his firm doing business with the city. The commission agreed unanimously that a commission investigation revealed insufficient evidence to show Rip violated the State Ethics Law, and recommended the case be closed against Williams.

Attorney General Charges Against Me

It was about 3 P.M. when the phone rang. A man identified himself as an investigator with the State Attorney General's Office. Someone had filed charges against me through an attorney. The investigator told me that he could not divulge names, even the attorney's. The charges were foolish and fuzzy. It claimed that I had given some grant money to another elected official that was funded for the purpose of working with "at risk" youths.

In a matter of two weeks, I received a letter stating that the matter was closed. There had been no wrongdoing on my part. The records were vindicative. The issue was created in the minds of the accusers. They hid their names, but I knew their motives and there are days when I am convinced that I also know their names, in spite of their clandestine activity.

It seemed that I was becoming a central player in this drama regardless of my desire to wait it out.

After I received word of my exoneration, I found my mind resting upon some advice given to me by my older sweet-spirited sister, Martha Patterson Smith, who said, "Horace, in the end the truth and goodness will always win out. You just have to pray for the grace to see it to the end." She was right.

Illegal Raises

As council members, we were bashed on the radio talk shows every day. It was the same group using the same strategies. It was uncomfortable, but it appeared to be contained. However, the circle grew wider as the council found itself in a quandary of employee legal issues.

In late October of 1993, sixteen employees of the Fire Department and three employees of the Parks and Recreation Department filed grievances with the Civil Service Board over raises that had been given to three employees. The raises had lifted each person more than $5,000 a year above the pay scale's limit for their jobs.

We asked attorney Jake Montgomery to review the matter. Jake's report was very disturbing. It indicated not only the existence of illegal raises given without city council approval, but also the possible production of false payroll reports to cover them up. According to Jake's report, testimony had been presented at the Civil Service Board's hearing that indicated that the city's personnel director had been given false computer printouts of payroll records for several months. Of course, this further indicated that a number of city employees were receiving less pay and benefits than they were actually being paid by the city. The council asked me to serve as liaison for personnel. I dropped by Mrs. Horn's office the day following the revelation.

"How did this happen?" I asked her.

She replied, "I really don't want to get anyone in trouble. I first noticed a red flare last December. I was looking at a payroll report that I guess I wasn't supposed to see."

"What troubles me is that this went into effect without council knowledge."

She leaned over her desk, pressed her hands beneath her cheeks, and said, "I hate to tell you, but a lot of things have gone into effect without council knowledge. During the past few months, a number of raises have been given, some with no documentation at all. I went to the mayor and he said it had been taken care of. In April, I was given paperwork saying the improper raises had been rescinded, but it was only a few days ago that I found out that the three people each continued to be paid at eleven dollars and sixty-two cents per hour. The mayor also told me later that he didn't give the raises. He asked me for a list of people who were outside their pay scales and I got it for him."

"I got printouts several times after that that showed the raises had been taken back. I was not allowed to see a printout from April 1992 to March 1993. When I started getting them again, they showed they were being paid at the same rate as they were being paid in December of 1991. The printouts that I received that showed the raises having been rescinded had the bookkeeper's code on them. In the past, it would only take fifteen to twenty minutes to get a printout, but later on it began to take a half-day to a day to get a printout. It never crossed my mind to ask if they were true and accurate."

I thanked her for her candor and directed her to turn the bogus reports over to the district attorney.

When asked about the bogus reports, the mayor said, "I contend that there are not any legitimate pay scales because the council has never adopted them by ordinance." He admitted writing the memo requesting the raises and said he had done so at the request of a council member. He also said that he was aware of the state law that prohibits a city from giving retroactive raises, and that he had given ten improper raises retroactively in 1991.

The Civil Service Board discovered a memo the mayor had sent to the bookkeeper saying the illegal raises should be taken back and the employees' pay should be adjusted to previous rates. The board also found that the mayor later gave verbal instructions to the bookkeeper telling her to contact him before each pay period to get the pay rate for the thirteen employees involved.

When Jake questioned the bookkeeper about the reasons why the raises were given without the council's approval or a written document approving them, the bookkeeper said, "My boss told me to do it and I do what he says." The mayor claimed that he never told the bookkeeper to disregard the memo, but said he did tell the bookkeeper to check with him every two weeks to make sure that the council and Civil Service Board had approved the raises.

As a result of that issue of credibility, the council lost confidence in the accounting and payroll procedures and reports. We took severe and immediate steps, which resulted first in a transfer and eventually a termination for that employee.

We were bashed that much more, even though the bookkeeper appealed the termination to Civil Service and lost. She finally appealed to the Alabama Court of Appeals, where she also lost. The facts meant little. We were pictured as being after the bookkeeper because the bookkeeper was loyal to the mayor. The fact that the bookkeeper apparently kept two sets of payroll records which involved illegal pay raises meant very little to those who were now calling for our resignations.

The grievances filed by the employees gave way to a full police investigation and a review of payroll and accounting practices to help insure the credibility of records and accounts. We as a council issued the following public statement: "Employees dealing with payroll and accounting records must be insulated from political influence and pressure. It is clear to the council this has not been the case and the current loss of credibility is a direct result. This current problem is yet another example of the problems the council had been confronted with due to the extraordinary situation facing our city. It is clear that without action by the council, these types of administrative problems will not be dealt with in the manner usual to other city governments."

I'd hoped that the council statement would be sufficient. I was wrong. The detractors went directly after me as liaison for personnel. The media pressed for a public statement and my supporters begged for a personal public statement. I finally responded by addressing the entire issue, because I knew that there were several more difficult decisions regarding personnel that confronted us. I began with the words of John F. Kennedy saying, "'Now the trumpet summons us again—not as a call to bear arms, though arms we need; not as a call to battle, though embattled we are; but a call to bear the burden of a long twilight struggle, year in and year out.' It is troubling, but it seems that we have had a scenario where pay raises were punched into the computer to give illegal pay raises, then an employee would go back into the computer and reprogram it to show the salaries without the raises that had been given. It appears to have been a deliberate intent to misguide. It will be sought to protect the integrity of our accounting practices in the future. There will be other personnel issues, but I ask that we go forth, even in this sad moment, rejoicing in hope, patient in tribulation, and showing up even on the most difficult of days."

A Clerk Who Took a Trip

While all the personnel issues were taking place, the police continued the Jerry Jackson investigation. Meanwhile, a revenue clerk billed the city for a trip to Montgomery, Alabama. The police department also continued the administrative investigation into the personnel issues. The clerk informed the detectives involved in the investigation that the trip was made at the mayor's request. When asked the nature of the trip, the clerk refused to give an answer. When reminded that the clerk was a probationary employee, the clerk walked away and said, "I am taking the Fifth."

The council president, Donald Hubbard, sent the clerk a letter instructing her to cooperate with Lieutenant Eugene Jacks in an investigation into compensation of city employees. Failure to give information would be considered a violation of a directive and an act of insubordination.

The clerk was paid for the two-day trip, but refused to answer questions about what was being done for the city on the trip. She only said that it was for the mayor and was confidential. The clerk was terminated and the circle of council-haters grew wider.

Two other city employees were terminated and we were accused of simply terminating people because of their political loyalty to the mayor. Even though we were confronted with serious issues escalating out of the official Civil Service hearing, many people just wanted the crisis at City Hall to go away. It would not.

Will B. Heard

Numerous letters, flyers, and brochures began to show up all over the city. These written instruments called for the council's resignation. Numerous charges were leveled against each of us. Taped to telephone poles, mailed in newsletters, passed out in supermarket parking lots, these inflammatory tracts made their way through the whole city. Each letter, flyer, and brochure was signed by a fictitious character by the name of "Will B. Heard."

District Attorney Robert Rumsey announced that he had begun a formal investigation into the Jerry Jackson case; he was subsequently assaulted with charges of corruption.

Literature was sent to churches, civic groups, elected officials, and the media. Tapes were also sent. Threats, innuendoes, and intimidation were used in the attempt to quiet the mayor's critics. Hitler proved that if you tell a lie long enough and no one confronts it, sooner or later, people will believe it. Will B. Heard was having a field day. As a council, we were taking body shots. Anyone who knows anything about boxing will tell you that blows to the body will eventually take their toll if you are in a fight for the long haul. We were.

The mayor began to use the local TV station. Day after day we took hits, until December 29, 1993. On December 28, 1993, the mayor was indicted by a federal grand jury on one count of fraud and twenty-eight counts of money laundering. The indictments came from the investigation launched from Rip Williams's formal request into payments made to the elusive tree-stump cutter, Jerry Jackson.

The news of the indictment was carried by the Associated Press and soon hit the airwaves throughout the state and nation. There were media representatives drawn to Talladega from far and near. The Jerry Jackson stump-remover story elicited a front page article from the *Wall Street Journal,* which appeared in its Wednesday, January 26, 1994 edition.

On the day after the mayor was indicted by the federal grand jury, the city council called a special meeting in order to educate the community on our position as a council body and inform them of matters that we felt appropriate. On December 29, 1993, at the request of my fellow councilmen, I shared a statement about all that had transpired, explaining our position as well as some of our past and future actions.

In the statement we admitted that the council had made several mistakes in judgment; that on many occasions, we had relied solely on information from Mayor Barton when we should have confirmed the information ourselves. We had also relied on an assumption that all city employees would disclose information to us when questionable activities were taking place. We had misjudged their loyalty and/or the possible pressure being applied to them. In many instances, our employees had not lied, but simply failed to keep us informed. The city had many dedicated and loyal employees and it was a major disappointment that a few had decided to serve a particular individual rather than the city.

The statement also attempted to explain some of the action we'd taken against several employees and assured citizens of Talladega that most of these employees had accepted their discipline and would continue to be city employees. Although elected as part-time officials, we acknowledged that we were remiss in not supervising our full-time employees better than we did, and assured the people of Talladega that we'd insure that procedures would change and that better accounting and payroll procedures would be implemented.

We asserted that we had tried to involve the mayor as much as he would let us, and that we had heard the pleas of our citizens to end the controversy. On each occasion in which we had attempted to involve the mayor, he had responded with another round of vicious and libelous personal attacks and/or a string of half-truths.

While this was a very difficult hour for our city, we were convinced that if we had yielded to the personal threats and attacks, the city would not have been served. We confronted a mayor who was popular, persuasive, and persistent. However, had we not accepted the responsibility to confront his activities and lack of leadership, the city would have faced a much bleaker day at some point in the future. We asked the people for their support, their advice, and their prayers during what we unfortunately expected to be a very disturbing time for our city.

The mayor was furious. He called a press conference and tore directly into me, saying that I was trying to be a big "boy." He also said, "Horace Patterson is running for public office and he's got to have an issue to take the heat off some of the things he's done in the past. We're not talking about Jerry Jackson. We're talking about some past employments."

The council responded in my favor, and expressed outrage at Barton calling me a "boy," a term that has long had racial overtones.

The mayor responded with, "If the shoe fits, wear it," and stated that he would not apologize. He went on to say, "If Horace Patterson knew what some of the black constituency calls him, he would be incensed."

In his anger, Barton had for the first time revealed the role he had assumed in seeking to control the African-American community. He had misread the votes that he had received from my ward. He, however, felt that those votes had endorsed him rather than come as a backlash over the Lawrence controversy. He further revealed his role in spreading the lies and filthy rumors concerning my past employment. When confronted, he would say, "This is what I heard." To his political advantage, Barton marketed himself as an expert on our community. He had toyed with African-Americans, but in a matter of a few months his public statements about Edythe Sims and about me began to erode the base that he had. And many black people who thought I had been too hard on him in the Vanessa Williams incident began to pick up on a dangerous theme in the life of a man many had called their friend.

Barton's attack on me was finally out in the open. Circumstances were as such that he knew that he could not survive as long as I sat in any seat of honor. It was him or me. The very fact that I could not be bought or intimidated meant that his political days of vote-getting with margins large enough to win the at-large mayor's office were over. I was able to articulate the issues. Feelings of unease were widespread, but the specific reasons behind them were vague even as I took notice of unfavorable changes in some black and white people who had called me friend for years. Some were simply afraid. They expected the coming venom and wondered if I could survive it. Many rallied to me. The situation between Barton and me was turning into an all-out war.

The Trial

U. S. Prosecutor Bill Barnett prosecuted the case. Barton pled not guilty. Prosecutor Barnett called numerous witnesses to establish that Barton bought and attempted to sell some real estate using the name

Wiley Gene Winters, as the property owner, rather than his own name. Barton's second cousin, Wiley Gene Winters, testified that he never had Barton perform any real estate transactions for him and never authorized Barton to use his name in a real estate transaction. When shown a copy of a lease-purchase agreement bearing the signature of Wiley Gene Winters, Barton's cousin testified that it was not his signature.

A number of Talladega bank tellers from Citizens Bank and First Alabama Bank testified that Barton cashed checks written to Jerry Jackson at their windows. They also testified that he often bought cashiers' checks or money orders in Jackson's name with proceeds from the cashed checks. Some of the checks had co-endorsements or signature verification signed by Barton. Included among the cashiers' checks, Barton purchased a 2,650 dollar money order used to buy real estate from a yarn mills manager by the name of Guy Kaylor.

Kaylor testified that Barton bought two residential lots from him using the name of Wiley Gene Winters. Kaylor said, "He told me that Winters was a trucker who lived in Bemiston and was in California at the time. He said he was just helping him out."

Blanche Ford was called. She testified that she bought one of the residential lots from Barton in 1993. She said that she took 1,000 dollars in 100 dollar bills to Barton's office to make a down payment on the property. She said that he had his secretary type up a lease-purchase agreement. He then took it into his office and a few minutes later he called her in. At that time, Winters's signature was on the paper.

Evidence was introduced by Barnett that included a 200 dollar payment on the property, which Barton wrote on the back of his business cards. The receipt was signed, "For Wiley Gene Winters by Larry Barton." The following month when her payment was due, Ms. Ford went to City Hall and told Barton that she wanted out of the deal because of the controversy over his association with Jerry Jackson. He refunded her money the next day.

City Hall employees Cindy Giddens, Carrie Curlee, and Becky Jenkins also testified that they had cashed Jackson's checks for Barton, but none had seen Jackson. "The checks were always endorsed before

Barton brought them in to be cashed," Ms. Giddens said.

"It was always between 4:30 and 5 in the afternoon. He would say Jerry Jackson was in his office and didn't have time to go to the bank," Ms. Curlee said.

Ms. Davis, of First Alabama Bank, testified that she sold a 699 dollar cashier's check to Barton that was sent to the Alabama Department of Revenue to buy a house on Hobson Avenue for back taxes in Jackson's name.

Mrs. Annie Lou Harris, the former owner of the Hobson Avenue property that Barton bought for 699 dollars and sold for 6,900 dollars, said she never signed a quit-claim deed on the property that Barton filed in the Talladega County Courthouse. She said she deeded the property over to an insurance company to settle a debt. She said that Barton had contacted her and told her the property needed to be cleaned up. When she told him it was no longer hers, he sent her a letter to sign that would relieve her of the responsibility. Mrs. Harris said, "When we got it in the mail, it was a quit-claim deed. We didn't sign it."

Prosecutor Bill Barnett presented the deed. It had a signature by Mrs. Harris and her husband.

She replied, "We didn't sign it. My husband was in Virginia at the time."

William Cooper, the man who paid Barton 6,900 dollars for the property, took the stand and stated that he had never met Jerry Jackson, but dealt with Larry Barton for the purchase and payment.

I was called to testify. The mayor had claimed that Jerry Jackson had removed stumps from an intersection in my ward. I testified that no stumps were removed, but city employees had cleared a thicket and cleaned out a ditch. John C. Burt, the property owner who lived at that intersection, echoed my testimony.

Barton had repeatedly told residents to "stay tuned." He had said that he had a surprise witness. It never happened. Barton declined to testify on his own behalf. The prosecution and the defense rested.

March 9, 1994

At 9:49 a.m., the U. S. district judge asked, "Ladies and Gentlemen, have you reached a verdict?"

"Yes, Your Honor," replied the jury foreman, Bruce Metzgar. He then handed twenty-seven signed verdict sheets to a court clerk, who in turn handed them to the judge. The judge flipped through the forms to make sure they were filled out and properly signed by the jury foreman. He passed the forms back to the clerk, and she read from each.

"We, the jury, find the defendant, Larry Barton, guilty as charged in count one . . . count two . . . count . . ."

Barton sat still.

Prosecutor Barnett raised his head, no doubt remembering his strong closing arguments:

> Ladies and gentlemen of the jury, the payments were made under the ruse of stump work. The money Barton took was made to look like it went to Jerry Jackson. Barton has no ethics and he has no moral turpitude. He was out to line his pockets at taxpayers' expense. He did it unabashedly and repeatedly. Jerry Jackson is in this courtroom. He stands before you in the form of Larry Barton. There's two sides to every story? Not when you're dealing with Larry Barton. There's what's happening and what he wants you to think is happening, and then "I didn't do it." It's your job to say, "Mr. Barton, we carry the checkbook."

On April 22, 1994, Barton was sentenced to fifty-one months in federal prison for fraud and money laundering. He claimed that his case would be overturned because the jury was all white. Barton, even at that moment, continued to try to use the black community as his personal tool and instrument for his personal benefit. It did not work.

The former mayor began his fifty-one-month sentence by reporting to Eglin Air Force Base in Florida. And with his departure, a new era began for our city.

Talladega Police Captain W. E. Hurst said, "It's been a difficult ten months. Although we've been subjected to ridicule and criticism, we've tolerated it and we've done our jobs."

U. S. Prosecutor Bill Barnett said, "Justice was served."

As for me, I found a beautiful illustration during the following days. The April rains hit and with them came the rainbows that speak their own messages of closure and new beginnings. The city was not simply reverberating with the aftershock of our ten-month ordeal, it was poised for a new and better chapter.

Donald Hubbard, the council president, was soon sworn in as mayor and with a packed council chamber, that ceremony unleashed a nervous excitement and a heady euphoria. Blood was coursing, adrenaline was pumping, and incredulity was rampant. A packed house at City Hall sent a clear message that our hopes would not be relegated to a world of private fantasy. The old had passed away. The new had come. None of us knew what the new would bring, but we were convinced that whatever it brought, the old had prepared us well to face it.

The ten-month ordeal had not hemmed me in. It had released me to explore new arenas. It had not broken me, it had undergirded and strengthened me to embrace the next challenge a bit wiser and convinced me that I, by the grace of God, could withstand the pressure and overcome any disappointment.

10

Leading and Learning

SOMETIMES THE BEST reaction to turmoil is to just let it run its course and wear itself down or out. There are other times when a failure to act is an invitation to disaster. Conceding today may be the best way to succeed tomorrow when it comes to some issues. However, a concession today in some of this life's hard places will assure that there will be no tomorrow. This life is not just one thing or one color. It is many things and a host of colors, from the bright and the bold to the fading and the flickering.

In the summer of 1994, I qualified as a candidate for the state legislature again. The district had been redrawn. It now covered two counties. I carried my home county of Talladega with 70 percent of the vote, but I lost badly in the other county. That county supported its own. The race was close, but when the dust settled, I had lost the election by thirteen votes. The loss was not heartbreaking, but it was disappointing. What made the race so discouraging were the tactics that were employed by some that I had befriended.

It happened one Friday evening about 7:30 p.m. Doe and I were channel surfing, and came to rest on the local T.V. station. A black man was being interviewed about the legislative race. He raised my name in the interview.

The interviewer, who was white, said, "I really like Dr. Patterson."

The black man responded, "What you need to know about him is that he doesn't really care about people. He has a bachelor's degree in psychology and a master's degree in counseling. He can psych people to make them think that he cares." The interviewer threw his head back as if he had been hit by a punch, then he quickly composed himself and moved on to another subject.

On the next day, the interviewer called me and apologized. He was a friend and said, "I don't know where that remark came from or why. It shocked me and I just want you to know that I'm sorry that it happened."

I thanked him for his kindness. I thought about the man who defined me as uncaring before a local T.V. audience. He had been one to whom I had loaned money, and I had even given money to his political aspirations. He had been the object of my generosity. He knew better. He was not some uninformed stranger whose assessment of me was built upon the whispers of my enemies. He was a man that had asked for my help in a needy time and had received it. I thought about the matter. I chewed on it, but I didn't swallow it.

Then it hit me like a ton of bricks. My leadership station had been enlarged in our city beyond my understanding. I didn't need the wings of a dove to fly away, I needed the wings of an eagle to fly above. Leadership is not easy. No person can go beyond the critics because problems are everywhere, but you can live above the critics even if you don't understand their motives. Regardless of what we've done for them, some people are happy to punish us in the areas that pain us the most, if they view us as having what they are missing. This is the price of leadership. This is the price for the appearance of success. It is not cheap and I have learned that if I consider the price too costly, I have no right to be considered a leader or defined as a success. Leadership is costly. It is not about wearing titles, it is evidenced in exerting influences in spite of critics and criticism.

Gossip can make news, but it cannot make history. I don't know where the definition came from, but I like it. One writer defined gossip as news you have to hurry and tell somebody else before you find out it isn't true. My life's story is one that is saturated with examples that teach against responding to rumors, gossip, and innuendoes. I have discovered that when you take care of your character, you can always trust God to take care of your reputation. Abraham Lincoln once said, "If I were to read, much less answer all the attacks made against me, this shop would close for business. I do my best; the very best I know how and the very best I can. I mean to keep on doing it until the end. And if the end brings me out wrong, then ten thousand angels swearing that I was right wouldn't make a difference."

Lincoln spoke true. I originally thought he was with this statement outlining the mentality of a successful leader, but now, after taking the risk and responsibility (refusing to play the role of the impala), I realize that Lincoln was speaking to the heart, not the head, of any person who feels the calling to be a leader. He understood, and made clear to me, that critics mean nothing in the larger picture of history, and that doing right, even when others say it is wrong, that is the true measure of a man's success as a leader and as a person. Some studies reveal that we forget 95 percent of what we've learned within seventy-two hours. Those facts might apply to details around some technical subject matter, but I doubt that they are appropriate to life on the experiential level as a leader.

There are some lessons too important to forget and too precious to dismiss. Leadership is not a popularity contest. At some point confrontation is required. Some people will hate you and some people will love you. Some people will deal you misery, and some people will deal you joy. But if you don't confront it the problems get worse.

I figure only those unwilling to take a stand are loved by everyone. To do right in the face of adversity, that is the only task that separates a strong leader from a good organizer. The price of leadership is great, but the privilege is special.

Leadership involves some suffering, but if you suffer correctly, the suffering is never wasted. Deserved or undeserved, suffering creates some of this life's most teachable moments. Leadership requires living for others and finding satisfaction in sacrifices that some will never appreciate. Leadership is honoring your own truth without honoring your own way as the only way. Leadership is sacrifice and heartache. Leadership is also reward and happiness.

Sometimes when our hands are full it is easy to forget some of the lessons that we learned when our hands were empty. Certificates of professionalism do speak well of excellence and they should be valued as emblems of honor, but the fact is too obvious for argument, that our certificates are dated. But time marches on and with its passion for change, knowledge continues to increase. The woman or man who sincerely seeks to lead others must humbly confess that she or he is in eternal need of augmented erudition.

This life is too short to waste any of it by being bitter. No leader can lead from a distance, but when you get close to some people you will get hurt. The erinaceus is a member of the hedgehog family. From a distance one cannot see the quills on it, but when you get close the quills spring out and pierce the skin. Some people seem harmless from a distance, but close up they sprout their quills and hurt you even when you are trying to help them. It is easy to write them off—there are times when you can't do anything but write them off. Yet there are other times when you must work on in spite of your personal pain. Some are good eggs, but are a little bit cracked. When you learn their background, instead of thinking about how far they have to go, you start to think that it is a miracle to see how far they have already come.

If you want to become a loser, all you have to do is carry a grudge. When people hurt you once and you fail to forgive them and refuse to move on, you allow them to keep hurting you every time you remember what they did. Human memory can become a kind of videotape in your heart, replaying reruns of a hurtful incident, bringing you pain each time it plays.

No race of people has a monopoly on good or evil. No denomination has the market on holiness. Both the sources and the systems of our lives are challenged daily and it seems to me that God is sometimes more concerned about what we can become than he is about what we are. Human relationships flourish and blossom not because guilty people are trounced, but because the innocent people are mercifully tolerant. There are some who cannot be trusted, but must not be trounced.

It seems easier to deal with the foul odor of deathly issues such as the base of interracial bitterness and the causes of racial chaos at a civilized distance, but the truth remains: it seems easy because it is not effective. You cannot deal with such profound problems of race relations from a distance. I am fully aware that there is a stench that escalates from anything that has been dead for any period of time. I think I can smell something coming from the intricate pile of race-related prejudice; it is not a pretty aroma.

Most will look away, but the leader who will truly make a difference in this inescapable arena is the one who patterns life after the God who never hides his face and who never covers his nostrils.

The future of our nation demands that we develop an understanding of the underlying factors that stubbornly resist remedy and constantly wreak havoc.

It was a Thursday afternoon in early spring, as an April shower gently bathed our English Tudor home, I sat alone in my office, located on the east end of our house, surrounded by the comforts of family photos depicting the growth of our children and the joys of pleasant memories. I was summoned back to the task at hand by the ringing of the telephone. I was greeted with a warm hello. It was the voice of Hattie Wallace, a lady of great charm whose spirit as a public educator is both attractive and engaging. She spoke, saying slowly, "I just wanted to call you and remind you that tall trees catch a lot of wind."

She laughed and went on to share with me some of her goals for our church usher board. I marveled at her unique ability to arrive at the heart of matters and recalled a time when she and Reverend Belvie Brice, a former associate minister in our church, who for the last ten years has meritoriously served as pastor of the Mount Zion Baptist Church in Birmingham, Alabama, shared that phrase with me.

There is a price to be paid by the soul that dares to tackle the entrenched evils of hatred and manipulation, but the price paid for confrontation is small compared to the cost of passivity. It takes some "tall trees,"—people with great insight, conviction, and courage—to make a marked difference in their age. They know misunderstanding and persecution, but they also become connective cells with that great nobility of good men and women who dance to the music that they know. Some are blessed with great formal training, while others are maybe not so well tutored but possess an extreme degree of intelligence and insight.

There is a Chinese proverb which says, "Learning is a treasure which follows its owner everywhere." What I have learned in leadership bears that truth's validity every single day. Because of this fact, I remain unbroken and unbound.

Index

A

Aaron, Hank   21
Abernathy, Ralph   43, 99
Alabama Association of School Boards   102–104, 106, 110, 111, 137
Alabama Baptist State Convention   41, 54
Alabama League of Municipalities   144
Allen, Monroe   128
Allen, Shirley   128
Anderson, Sharon   107
Armstrong, Daniel B.   68
Armstrong, Imogenge   92
Ashley, Henry   131
Askew, Willie   47

B

Baker, Ossie   129
Baker, Walter   59, 66, 74–75
Barnett, Bill   167, 184, 188
Barney, Edison Daniel   105, 118
Barton, Larry   80–83, 139–142, 143–148, 144, 149, 157–158, 161, 163–188
BBC   82
Beavers, Alberta   132
Beavers, Ronnie C.   114
Bellingrath, Walter   138
Bessemer Rough Rocks   15, 18
Birmingham Black Barons   15
Blacksher, James U.   121
Bledsoe, Lillie   129
"Bloody Sunday"   42–43
Blount, Billy   24–25
Bolden, Simpson   132
Bolden, Yvonne   132
Booker, Lee   16
Boswell, Clarence   46
Bragg, Rufus   171
Bray, Bernard   65
Brown, Mary Lou   128
Buchanan, George   128
Buchanan, Katrina   124–126, 128, 134
Buffalo Recess   98
Bunche, Ralph   43
Burbons   40–41, 53, 71
Burke, Edmund   66
Burt, John C.   186

C

Calhoun, Wren   128
Cameron, Sandra   68
Canaan Estates II   98
Canady, Ella   129
Canady, Willie   131
Carmichael, Stokely   115
Carter, Nathan   45
Carzello, John   118
Castleberry, Annie   129
Chiapel, Tom   81
Churchill, Winston   123
Clark, Johnny   93
Clark, Louis   128
Clark, Sadie   128
Clemons, U. W.   135
Cobb, Sara   66
Cochran, Daisy   127
Cokely, Eula   66

Cokely, William   58
Coleman, Annette   130
Colley, John   130
Community Life Institute   67
Connor, Bull   25
Cook, Nathan   115
Cooper, Alma   131
Cooper, William   165–167, 186
Cotton, Percy   130
Curlee, Carrie   185
Curry, Catherine   129
Curry, Frank   133
Curry, Jerome   68
Curry, Myrtis   130
Curry, Rosa   130
Curry, Sharon   130

D

da Vinci, Leonardo   139
Dark, J. C.   171
Dark, Joe   171
Dark, Rufus   171
Davis, Margaret   130
Dawson, B. W.   90
Dexter Avenue Baptist Church   54
Dortch, Clarence   114, 130
Dortch, Floretta James   114, 130
Dortch, Peggy   114
Douglas, Charon   131
Douglas, Gerald   131
Draper, Deneen   128
Draper, Harold   128
Dubois, W. E. B.   98

E

Ebony magazine   56
Edmund Pettus Bridge   42

F

Falkenberry, John C.   121
Fielding, Jerry   153

Flanningan, Freddy   115
Fleming, Betty   130
Ford, Blanche   185
Foster, Harold   128
Foster, James D.   176
Foster, Jan   128
Fowler, Ed   169
Fuller, Myrtle   130

G

"gang of nine"   73–77, 95
Garner, Peggy   128
Garner, Sylvester   128
Garret, Mary   129
Garrett, Carol   130
Garzarelli, Bernadette   154
Ghandi, Mahatma   43
Giddens, Cindy   185
Good Hope Church   58
Grace, Jamie   163
Graham, Patricia   68
Greater Ebenezer Baptist
   Church   114
Green, Cora   130
Gresham, Quinten   65

H

Hamlin, Mike   159, 171
Hardy, Tommy   115
Harris, Bobby   44–45, 116
Harris, Brenda   116
Harris, Johnny   93, 118
Harris, Laura   118
Hartley, Jerry   105
Haskins, Henry   44–45
Hawkins, Marshall   128
Hawkins, Vivian   128
Henderson, Clarence   114
Hicks, Beecher   97
Hollingsworth, Hosea   46
Hollingsworth, Lizzie   46

Horn, Sue   159, 161, 178
Houston, J. D.   132
Hubbard, Donald   152, 168, 173, 174, 181, 188
Huff, Ozzie   52
Hughes, Langston   110
Hurst, Steve   140
Hurst, W. E. "Pee-Wee"   158, 168, 172, 187

J

Jackson, Andrew   60
Jackson, Arthur   74–75
Jackson, Hazel   128
Jackson, Jerome   128
Jackson, Jerry   153, 157–158, 163, 164–188, 165
Jackson, Jessie   150
Jacobs, L. L.   115
James, Louise   129
James, Sylvester   127
Jelks, James   171
Jenkins, Becky   185
Jenkins, Emily   130
Jenkins, Terran   130
Jeter, Patricia   24
Johns, Vernon   54
Johnson, Coronad   35–36, 37, 74
Johnson, Eunice   56
Johnson, Henry Louis   105
Johnson, Joseph Henry   61
Johnson, Larry   30–31
Johnson, Lyndon   43
Johnson, Minnie   129
Jones, Jerry   115
Jones, Walter   115
Jordan, Mary   19, 20, 32
Jordon, Curtis   18, 21, 32
Junior Welfare League   109

K

Kansas City Monarchs   21
Kaylor, Guy   185
Keith, André   116
Keller, Helen   133
Kelley Springs Baptist Church   115
King, Julian   140
King, Martin Luther Jr.   27–28, 43, 55, 86, 99, 115
Kirkland, Reo   122
Kirsey, Bettye   58
Kirsey, Carolyn   58
Ku Klux Klan   41, 71, 141

L

Lawler, Johnny   128
Lawler, Rose   128
Lawrence, Lillian   106
Lawrence, Thomas Y.   65, 101–142, 141
Leonard, Matthew   115
Liberty Baptist Church   51
Lippmann, Walter   137
London Times   82
Lowery, Joseph   107
Lucas, Faye   132
Lucas, Wiley   132
Lynch, Willie   71–72

M

Mabra, B. N.   67
Manzie, Charles   46
Marshal, Daisy   48
Marshall, Daisy   47
Marshall, Eddie   47
Maxwell, Mildred   93
McApine, William   56
McGhee, Henry   116
McGraw, Lawrence   118, 128
McGraw, Maenola   118, 128

McIntosh, Dolia. *See also* Patterson, Doe
   marrying Horace Patterson 51
McIntosh, Marion 86
McKenzie, Clarence 127
McKenzie, Nellie 127
McKinne, Johnny 114
McKinney, B. E. 109, 114, 117
Metzgar, Bruce 187
Mfume, Donald 79
Mfume, Keith 79
Mfume, Kweisi 79
Miller, Ray 107
Mills, Billy 102
Montgomery, George 91, 92
Montgomery, Jake 152, 169, 175–176, 178
Moody, D. L. 57
Moore, Dale 131
Moore, Walter 130
Morrison, Edmund 133
Mount Canaan Baptist Church 56, 62–63, 65, 69, 72, 77, 98
Mount Cleveland Baptist Church 115

N

National Basketball Association 100
New Saint Paul Baptist Church 38
New Saint Paul Church 22
Niemoller, Martin 66
Nix, Mary 129
Notes on the Alabama Constitution of 1901 40

O

Orr, Francis 129

P

Parks, Rosa 102
Patterson, Doe 52, 55, 56, 65, 71, 80, 84, 87, 90, 109, 118, 119, 126, 132, 189
   as candidate for School Superintendent 137
Patterson, Hattie 130
Patterson, Horace
   as a young adult 15–21
   as pastor of Liberty Baptist 51–53
   as pastor of Mt. Canaan Baptist 56–60, 63–77
   at Selma University 41–46
   battling Larry Barton 164–188
   called to preach 26–32
   fighting for Dr. Lawrence 103
   first sermon 33–34
   in the Air Force 34–40
   living in Talladega 60–62
   looking forward 189–193
   marrying Dolia McIntosh 51
   meeting Dolia McIntosh 48–50
   on board of education 78–100
   running for City Councilman 127–133
Patterson, Horace Jr. 51, 57, 81, 90, 91, 118, 132, 138
   birth of 56
Patterson, Ivy 89
Patterson, Ivy Eleece 51, 122, 132
Patterson, Jay 51
Patterson, John 25
Patterson, Julian Niles 90, 91, 118, 132, 138
   birth of 72
Patterson, Mary Ann 32
Paul Hill Tigers 15
Peasant, Emma 129
Peasant, George 56
Pettus, Clarence 143, 146
Phillips, Fannie Mae 127
Pinkston, Martha 129

Player, Eddie   64
Player, Marie   128
Pugh, Thomas   128

R

Ratcliffe, Essie   46
Reaves, Annette   128
Reeves, Ed   128
Rembert, Stanley   131
Rhoden, Flora   92
Rocky Mount Baptist Church   114
Rogers, Ron   108
Roosevelt, Theodore   139
Rowls, Lester   130
Rumsey, Robert   160, 162, 182

S

Savery, William   61
Sawyer, David   105, 118
Scales, Patricia   131
Seals, Jack   94
Selocta   60
Shady Grove Baptist Church   114
Shoemaker, Wallace   67
Sims, Edythe   105, 110, 149–154, 157, 175, 184
Sims, Horace   128
Sims, Shirley   128
Sims-deGraffenried, Dr.   103, 105
Sinclair, Denise   122
Sisk, Ken   158, 164, 168, 172
Sixteenth Street Baptist Church bombing of   25
Smith, Betty   18
Smith, J. T.   98
Smith, Martha Patterson   177
Southern Christian Leadership Conference   99, 107
Spratlin, James   159
Spruill, Herman   57
Spurgeon, Charles Haddon   131

Steele, David   47
Still, Edward   121
Storey, Barbara   128
Storey, James   128
Stowers, Eddie   162
Strickland, Frank   93, 106, 109, 113, 117
Strickland, Rosa   92
Sutton, Don   97
Swain, Maude   130
Sykes, Susie   131

T

Talladega Citizens for a Better Society   109, 118
Talladega County Democratic Conference   117
Talladega Daily Home   107, 111, 169
Tarrant, Thomas   61
Teague, John   65
Thomas, Josie   117
Thomas, Julia   66
Thomas, Julius   124–126
Thompson, Bobbye   131
Threatt, Stanley   115
Threatt, William   115
Townsend, Charles   105
Truss, Juanita   131
Tubbs, Patricia   132
Tubbs, Robert   132
Tucker, Eddie   106, 110, 111, 118, 124–126, 128
Tucker, Meriam   128
Tunstall, Charles A.   90
Turner, Jo Ann   129
Turner, Samuel   114
Twenty-Four Horsemen   62

U

Urquhart, Bessie Beck   98

V

Voting Rights Act of 1965   43, 134

W

Walker, Felicia   132
Wall Street Journal   80, 182
Wallace, George   25
Wallace, Hattie   128, 193
Wallace, Wilby   74, 92, 128
Whatley, Joe   121
Whatley, Willis   164
Wiersbe, Warren   63
Wiggins, Bobbie   129
Wiggins, Roy   131
Williams, Howard   150
Williams, Rip   153, 156, 165, 173, 176, 182
Williams, Vanessa   80–83, 91, 140
Willoford, John   73–75
Wilson, A. W.   54
Wilson, Byrd   30–31
Wilson, Git   20, 21
Wilson, Jerry   157, 165
Winters, Wiley Gene   185
Woodruff, Hale   61
Wright, Gussie   39–41, 52, 71

Y

Young, Columbus   128
Young, Ludie   128

www.ingramcontent.com/pod-product-compliance
Lightning Source LLC
Chambersburg PA
CBHW022100160426
43198CB00008B/298